Dee,

Happy
        Birthday!
With love and
th

D1304350

2007

Sacred Spaces

PARACLETE PRESS

sacred spaces

STATIONS ON A CELTIC WAY

MARGARET SILF

Published in the United States in 2001 by
Paraclete Press
Brewster, Massachusetts
www.paracletepress.com
ISBN   1-55725-278-5

Text copyright © 2001 Margaret Silf

The author asserts the moral right
to be identified as the author of this work

Original edition published in English
under the title *Sacred Spaces* by
Lion Publishing plc
Sandy Lane West, Oxford, England
www.lion-publishing.co.uk
© Lion Publishing plc 2001

All rights reserved.
No part of this book may be reproduced
in any form or by any means without the prior
written consent of the publisher, except in brief
quotations used in reviews.

Typeset in 11/14 Berkeley Oldstyle
Printed and bound in Singapore

Contents

THE SPIRIT OF THE WAY

'Humankind has lost its way.' This sentiment surfaces frequently in our age, and sometimes it does feel as though everything is falling apart around us – not just in our personal crises, but, increasingly, in what feels like a shake-up of all our collective certainties. The structures that have held us more or less together in recent centuries no longer hold. National, cultural and religious identities are no longer absolute. Physics and mathematics are venturing into the same oceans of uncertainty. Ethics and morality are in a turmoil of contradictions and dilemmas.

So have we really lost our way? Or have we just mislaid it for a while? Has our 'way' perhaps become buried underneath all the complications we have constructed on top of it?

This book is an invitation to explore a 'way' – a Celtic Way. If we burrow down into the earth of our human spiritual experience and searching, we come across the traces of many 'ways'. In Judaism, the children of Israel followed the way out of slavery, through the deserts of experience, to the Promised Land. Islam regards the pilgrimage to Mecca as one of the five pillars of faith. The Buddhists seek the Way to Enlightenment. Chinese spirituality expresses the paradox of the journey in the Tao. The first Christians were known as the People of the Way, and Jesus identified himself as the Way. In modern physics too, fixed certainty is giving way to an understanding of life as a process, in which every part interacts with every other part, and everything profoundly affects everything else.

It seems, then, that in ancient as in modern times, the human heart has always been looking for a way. But a way to what? What are we actually looking for? Where or who is the destination? If we look back over several thousand years of organized religion we will find a plethora of answers – some of them very definitive – to that question. We have defined 'heaven' in almost as much detail as we have mapped out the Earth. There are those who will tell us just how many mansions it contains and who may enter them, and precisely what we must do to get an entry permit.

The spirit of the Way will not allow us to pitch camp and stay for ever with these artificial certainties. The spirit of the Way is much simpler, and more challenging than that. The plants and animals and even our small children know, with a wisdom deeper than ours, that the Way is simply about growing and becoming whoever we really are, in the core of our being. It is about recognizing the acorn in our hearts and trusting the process by which it will become an oak. It is about cooperating with that process of Becoming, about keeping our feet on the earth of our own lived experience, even as we reach out to the horizon beyond us. And it is about letting our own personal Becoming be fully engaged with the evolution, physical, intellectual and spiritual, of the whole of creation.

This book is written in the spirit of the Way. It follows a path that was walked by one branch of the human family, in the Celtic regions, in the early centuries after the life of Christ, but it also resonates with, and reveres, the spiritual quest of all humankind, since life on earth began. Institutional Christianity has built many a solid edifice on top of this path, but not so much as to obliterate its traces. Now, as some of those edifices are starting to break down, more and more spiritual journeyers are seeking out these neglected pathways and discovering, in joy, that they are ways which can be trusted, ways of deep simplicity that truly lead them closer to the heart of themselves and the heart of creation.

The 'way' is a journey, not a structure. It is a process of growth, not a system of salvation. It has many faces, of which the Celtic face is but one. And the Celtic Way itself has many facets. This book explores just one way of travelling a Celtic Way. It invites you to spend a little time in seven 'sacred spaces'. And, as you pause to reflect on your experience, it invites you to weave your own story into the story of creation, and to let your own dreams and desires rise up, like the Celtic cross, to join the earth you live on to the heaven you strive for. This Prologue will point towards a few signposts for such a journey. The rest of the book is a place of encounter, sacred and unique to you and your

Becoming, a place where the invisible and the visible, in yourself and in all creation, can become reconnected.

For the Celts there was never any shadow of doubt that these two worlds, the visible and the invisible, the material and the spiritual, were one. In every way the visible and the invisible were interwoven, as surely as the air we breathe and the food we eat come together to give life to our bodies. The invisible was separated from our sense perceptions only by the permeable membrane of consciousness. Sometimes that membrane could seem as solid as a brick wall. Sometimes it could seem very thin. Indeed, we speak even today of some places as being 'thin places', meaning that the presence of the invisible and the spiritual in those places is almost palpable.

Our Celtic forebears revered such 'thin places' as 'sacred space'. They sensed intuitively that here the visible world was totally interpenetrated by an invisible world which is mystery, yet which is somehow in relationship with us. Sacred spaces reflect these guiding insights of Celtic spirituality:

● They are stations on our personal journey towards our wholeness – places where we stand still, in awe, where the barrier between our time-bound and our eternity-seeking selves is lowered.

● They are sacraments – they encapsulate something of the mystery towards which they point, and they help to make this mystery real and incarnate in our human lives.

● They invite us to experience glimpses of transcendence and help us to live our everyday lives in the light of the vision of a reality beyond ourselves.

● They are personal to each of us, but they are the space in which we are drawn to an inclusive wholeness where we are all one in unity. They are places of community, sacred for each, sacred to all.

● They speak to our hearts personally, as a friend might speak. They are not doctrinal, but *experiential*. They draw us into deeper community with each other, with the whole circle of creation, and with a creating power who holds all in being and desires to be in relationship with every creature.

We might even imagine this invisible 'membrane' as a kind of spiritual ozone layer. Sometimes the intensity of our own emotion or depth of experience seems to burn a hole in this layer and let the brilliance of an eternal reality shine through. Sometimes it seems to be the other way round, and the invisible, the divine, breaks through to us, as it were, from beyond the veil, in ways we did not expect and cannot either predict or understand.

Sacred space, whether it has a geographical location or whether it is a space within our own experience, has special power. It has the ability to move us forward towards some new growth in our Becoming. It holds a call towards transcendence, if we have ears to hear.

Space can become sacred, for example, when it is saturated in prayer, perhaps because it has been a place of retreat and reflection for prayerful pilgrims through the centuries. It might be an island of Iona in sacred history, or an island of prayer in our own daily lives. Or it may be space that has been charged with an intensity of emotion, either of great joy or deep grief. An ancient battleground on the map, perhaps, or a place in our memory where a personal dream has been done to death. Or it may be a place or an inner experience that has been 'touched by eternity'. Some natural locations have this kind of quality. Near my own home, for example, is a hilltop with a cluster of houses forming an old village community. The cottages seem to be soaked in their own invisible history, and the sky feels so very close in that place, with a clarity that can be breathtaking. And most of us have memories of moments when we too were held in an experience of timelessness and wonder. On our Celtic Way we will pause at seven stations of sacredness, and make our own connections about what they might mean for us. Each of these places or symbols was revered as sacred in Celtic spirituality:

- *The infinite knot*, weaving wholeness out of partialness, and simplicity out of complication;

- *The high cross*, connecting Earth and heaven, our facts and our dreams;

- *Hilltops*, offering us the vision of what might be and the inspiration to follow the vision;

- *Wells*, taking us to the depths of our experience to find the treasure in our shipwrecks;

- *Groves and springs*, giving us the support of community, and inspiring new life and new hope;

- *Crossing places*, such as causeways, bridges and burial grounds, inviting us to go beyond our present limits;

- *Boundaries*, where the cutting edge of growth and change is encountered.

This book will take us deep into personal sacred space. But it is not a travel guide for a personalized ego trip (which would have been anathema to the Celtic mind) because when we go deep into our own sacred space, we move closer to the centre and heart of all creation. There we encounter each other, and the eternal presence in which we are held. We discover a web of interrelatedness that calls us into a unity which defies the kind of separateness and estrangement from each other in which many of us live our lives today.

Woven into this exploration of sacred spaces is the thread of our own story, told in the various chapters, or stages of our lives. Each of the 'stations' on the journey through the book reflects something of one of the successive stages of our living and searching, though, of course, our life stages are never as regular or consistent as this might imply. On the contrary, they weave their own patterns, sometimes leaping forward, sometimes winding back upon themselves and re-emerging in a new place, in a new way, like the intricacies of the Celtic knot.

Broadly, however, we might identify seven stages or 'seasons', which we all experience in our own time and our own way:

- *Beginnings*, in the weaving of our being, physical and spiritual, in our earliest days and years;

- *Times of commitment* to quest after our own inner truth, and to live true to what we discover;

- *Seasons of setting out*, with vision and hope, upon new ventures, into new relationships, and upon our personal vocations;

- *Turning, and returning* to our truth and our deepest sources, when we feel we have lost our way;

- *Seasons of companionship* and the communion of intimate friendship, giving us the experience of Belonging;

- *Times of transition*, when we are commissioned to enter upon the unknown with courage and with trust;

- *Boundary seasons*, where we walk the edges of human experience, illumined by the vision of a fullness of life beyond our finite imagination.

These patterns and stages of growth weave in and out of our experience. We often feel a desire to mark them ritually or sacramentally, in 'rites of passage', shared in community. And so each chapter reflects on these sacramental rites and invites you to discover your own ways of marking them.

The stations along this Celtic Way will frequently invite you to stop for a while and go into your own inner space for reflection. For some people this is a regular part of their pattern of life. For most, however, life leaves us little if any time for calm collectedness like this. Nevertheless, the journey will not unfold itself to the full unless we take time to stand back and become aware of who we really are, as often as circumstances permit.

These are two ways that I have found help me personally to reach an oasis of calm from time to time. You might like to try them, or discover the ways that work for you:

- Remember a place and a time when you felt very much at peace, at home, warm, held, connected or loved. Just recall the details of the experience. Use your senses to help you. What could you see, hear and feel? Let every detail come to mind and just relive the experience in the here and now. Don't try to analyse your feelings. Simply let them be there, as if you were immersing yourself in a favourite video. Let this memory be like a little room in your mind, to which you can return whenever you wish. Let it be a sacred space.

- As you go through the day's tasks and activities, stop now and then, even if only for a moment, and let yourself become wholly aware of what you are doing. Hold the wood or metal you are working with and simply revere the fact that it is there, yielding to your work and creativity, part of the same creation as yourself. Be aware of the pottery and china as you wash up. Feel the texture of your clothes. Really taste and savour the food you eat, the water, the wine, the bread and the fruit. Stand in the garden or the park and notice the trees and the flowers, look up at the sky, listen to a bird singing, stroke your dog or cat, but do these things with your whole attention. Become aware of the ground you walk on, the grass and the stones, the wooden floors or the tarmac roads. Feel the bumps. Notice the differences. Smell the air. Smell the changing seasons. To be totally aware of the present moment is at the heart of all meditative practice. It gives us a hotline to the core of our being.

This is a journey for all who have ever experienced a glimpse of eternity slanting down through the clouds of everyday. However, my own 'way' is a Christian one, and I use Christian language and images where I feel these might be helpful. In every chapter there are imaginative retellings of biblical stories to help in the exploration of our sacred spaces. You may have rejected the flawed attempts by organized religion to take hold of this mystery. Or you may have formalized your intuition of the mystery in an explicitly Christian context, or that of any other faith. Either way, I invite you to receive these stories afresh, as once you listened to the stories your parents told you, with disbelief suspended, to make room for a sense of wonder.

Jesus described himself as the Alpha and the Omega – the source and the destination of all that is. Christians believe Jesus is God's 'sacred space' – one in whom the transcendent creator interpenetrated the created world in human form. We also believe the Christ-life is being lived out through time, energized and directed by the Holy Spirit, until every life has been lived and every death has been died. This is the scale of the journey. From Alpha to Omega. From Jesus of Nazareth to the Cosmic Christ. From time to eternity. Through Becoming to Being. From your acorn to your oak tree and from your oak tree to the forest of all creation.

For all of us, the only beliefs to which our deepest heart and soul can consent are those which our personal experience endorses. Sacred spaces are opportunities to meet that experience and allow it to take us beyond itself. And then to discover for ourselves what the mystery we call life means for us and where it is drawing us.

CHAPTER I

THE INFINITE KNOT

THE WEAVING OF THE DREAM

*I*t is remarkably difficult to follow a single thread through the intricacies and convolutions of one of the infinite-knot patterns, which are so much the hallmark of our Celtic heritage. If you try, you may find that your mind becomes occupied, as if by a mantra, leaving your deeper consciousness more open to the whispers of eternity. It can be even more difficult to follow the knotted threads of our own lives and feelings without losing sight of the balance in which they are ultimately held. More difficult, but even more liberating.

The knot holds us in a state of suspended contradiction. We know, with our minds, that we are finite. We are born. We live our span of years. And we die. The knot contradicts this knowledge with its statement of endlessness, and in our deeper reaches something knows that this, too, is true. Something in the depths of us is unending – or at the very least it is intimately joined to a reality that is unending.

With our minds we know our lives are a mass of complication. If you think back to yesterday, or forward to tomorrow, you will surely become aware of a whole catalogue of problems, dilemmas, choices and compromises, beaten into some kind of shape on the anvil of your circumstances. A far cry from the perfect balance of the infinite knot. Yet in your deeper reaches there are whispers of simplicity, harmony, a joining of opposites, a reconciliation of irreconcilables.

These deeper reaches are not the realms of fantasy. They are sending signals to us from layers of our being that lie below the conscious mind's domain. If they were not real, with real power to transform, then our psyche would not be registering any interest in these symbols of infinity, such as the Celtic knot. As it is, however, the knot fascinates us, just as it fascinated our forebears, and it draws us ever more deeply into itself. It speaks to us of:

● Complexity held in a greater simplicity;

● Limitation held in limitlessness;

- Partialness held in wholeness;

- Ourselves held in something infinitely greater than ourselves.

Can such a place of paradox become a sacred space within us, guiding us to a deeper discovery of who we really are, who we are becoming, and in what wholeness we are all held?

Islands of disconnection

I work from home. This means that I spend most of my working hours using the computer on my desk, doing the things I am asked to do; and when I need to, I dial in to my employer's office via a telephone line. I use the phone to connect me to the information I need from the office. Without this link I would not be able to do my job.

As you can imagine, this kind of interconnection is all a bit flimsy and superficial. The phone connection can fail, and it does from time to time. Then all I get on my computer screen is the helpful message that I have suffered a 'fatal termination'! Or, even more commonly, I find myself in no man's land because there is a power cut.

Working like this helps me to realize I am an 'island' for most of the time, and what I do only makes sense when I am 'reconnected' to the invisible world at the other end of the telephone line. But, far more seriously, I am an island in a deeper, less obvious way. I live most of my waking life in a world I might call 'consciousness'. It is my personal world, and I am its centre of gravity. I can very easily start to imagine that this world of mine is *the* world, and that all creation should be in orbit around *my* centre of gravity.

Deeper down, my unconscious depths know that there is an invisible 'beyond'. They know it from dreams, from prayer and from silent glimpses of a wisdom not my own. But my conscious self can, all too often, insist on its own self-sufficiency. When this happens I become disconnected. My conscious and unconscious selves fall into a state of contradiction, and I feel torn between the two. I live in a state of fragmentation. Perhaps this is the source of much human pain and tension.

These thoughts take me back to the memory of a place that is very close to my heart – the Western Isles of Scotland. I have stood there on the hills of the mainland and gazed out over the sea, dotted with islands, large and small, green and barren, smooth and rocky. From some points of view there appear to be hundreds of islands and rocky outcrops, as if some giant had dropped a bag of jewels in the sea. At dawn or at sunset they shine like diamonds. In stormy weather they strike terror into the hearts of seafarers, as their craggy teeth reach up from the waters to seize unwary craft and suck them down to destruction.

Even if you are not familiar with this part of the world, you will probably have known islands of your own, or you will be able to imagine our world in the way we see it when we look at its outer surface – an expanse of oceans, dotted with land masses, large and small, continents and islands. It isn't difficult to take this imagined scene further and realize that we human beings live our lives on these land masses. We are all islanders. Some of our islands are huge continents, and we lose our sense of living on an island. For those of us who live in the British Isles, however, the sense of being islanders is never far below consciousness, and indeed, so we are often told, we tend to be much more 'insular' than our 'continental' neighbours.

Our island view of things can easily cut us off from each other by focusing on the tides that divide us from others. However, it also carries the gift of inviting us to ponder the reality *below* the tides. Let us return for a moment to that island vista we might see from the Celtic coastlands. Imagine the islands spread out all around you. Imagine your own life as if it were an island, and notice how that forms your view of the islands around you. Your 'reality' is defined by your island. Other people live on their own islands and have their own 'reality'. You may be able to connect to them in various ways. You can make contact with them, for example, by using a boat, or even by building a bridge. You can do business with them, or exchange friendly communications. Or you can make war on them and hurl missiles at them.

Humankind knows a great deal about how to carry on this inter-island communication. We all do it all the time. Each of us is our own island and we spend much of our waking time trying to communicate with each other's islands. We do it personally, and we do it collectively, as communities, nations or ethnic or religious groupings, for example. We call it 'dialogue', and it is essential to our humanness, just as my ability to communicate with my employer by the telephone link is essential to my ability to do the job. And, like the islands off the craggy Scottish coast, our human islands can also be a focus of joy and wonder in our life's journeying, for example, when we experience love. Or they can be the cause of our shipwrecks, when we collide with each other in the dark. Whatever our relations with our fellow islands, however, one thing is clear – we are dealing on the surface of things. We may relate to each other in all kinds of ways, but as long as we remain islands, we can never know the deeper reality of each other. It simply isn't visible or tangible, and it can't be guessed at. Islands and continents are a surface view of our Earth. In the same way they provide only a surface view of ourselves and of each other.

One below the tideline

But now let your imagining go a little further. As you gaze at these islands – the physical islands of a remembered coastline, and the human islands with whom you are in daily contact – just let the tide go out, universally. If this were to happen, it would become instantly obvious that the deeper reality is very different. The reality below the tideline is not a set of disconnected islands and continents at all, but a single lump of rock, spinning through space. We call it the Earth. It is the bedrock of our being, and our islands and continents are just passing pimples on its surface.

Might not the same be true of our inner islands? Consciously we live our lives as if the centre of gravity were in our personal island. This is the way we survive as living, physical, conscious beings. But unconsciously, as any psychologist will tell us, there is a largely unexplored bedrock of common ground, and of deep unity. Physicists, too, are telling us that every particle of creation is interconnected with every other particle. Sometimes we catch glimpses of this bedrock unity – in inexplicable memories or intuitions, in dreams, or in meditative prayer. Sometimes we know we are touching the bedrock when we experience a moment of deep communion or empathy with another human being, or even with an animal, or when we catch the wonder of creation, in a starlit night or a dew-filled dawn, a baby's touch or the dying breath of a loved one.

All this leads me to the conclusion that most of the life of which I am consciously aware is being lived at the island level, spinning round a centre of gravity which is misleading, and potentially dangerous. At a deeper level I sense there is a need to be reconnected, and guided by a centre of gravity that lies not in my 'ego-self', but in the bedrock where all of creation is held in unity, and where my own true self subsists. This deep unconscious need expresses itself in my desire to 'belong'. Occasionally I am in touch with this bedrock. Perhaps someone looks into my eyes and sees my heart. Perhaps creation itself speaks to me in a language that makes me long to respond with joy to a touch, once known, but lost. When such things happen, I am reminded of my longing to be permanently connected to the wholeness of creation, and to be an integral part of it. The realization of this longing keeps me moving on and searching. It keeps me on the pilgrimage of life.

These reflections have taken me several pages, and quite a struggle, to put into words. The Celts, however, managed to do this in just a single picture – the picture of the infinite knot. Before you read on, you might like to pause for a few minutes and simply gaze at the picture of the knot on page 15, in the light of the possibility that there may be a deeper centre of gravity to our being than the one we cherish in our own ego-selves.

This intuition of things not understood, and realities not quite arrived at, is nothing new. It has been part of our human questing since the first stirrings of human consciousness. This is how our earliest ancestors discovered the pain of disconnection. What follows is a retelling of part of the book of Genesis. It is the story of Adam and Eve, who are the archetypes of ourselves in our first beginnings. Adam and Eve begin their existence in a state of oneness and harmony with God their creator and with all creation. The story goes on, however, to describe their experience of losing this harmony when, tempted by the promises of a serpent, they disobey God's instructions, and eat fruit from a tree he has forbidden them to touch. It tells, in the form of a story, a truth that we can feel, if we let ourselves, deep in the heart of our own experience.

It is one of the great sorrows of modern life that we rarely listen to the inner voice which so often speaks in pictures and symbols. In our frenzy to keep the island life in order, we dismiss the possibility of the vast underwater world across which we ply our little boats of consciousness. The story of Adam and Eve begins while they are still in touch with the bedrock reality of that underwater world and shows the consequences of losing that connectedness. Their truth comes to us across the aeons. We dismiss it at our peril.

The created world was in its infancy. Nothing was growing. Evolution had not yet begun. There was no rain falling from above, but there was a spring of water coming up from the depths, from the bedrock. This was the water that flowed out over the earth to set in motion the whole pageant of creation. The elements, those basic building blocks of creation, were all present in the first crescendo of fire that we call the Big Bang. They were present in the earth. God took this earth, these same basic elements, and wove them into the fabric of life. These same elements from interstellar space became the elements of the human body. The same energy that had set the process of creation in motion became the breath of life, and the desire for growth that animates every living thing.

From these two sources, the elements of the earth and the living stream of water, life evolved, and the breath of desire flowed through it all and made it live!

It was the garden of original wholeness, and in that wholeness all living things were in bedrock union with the source of their being, whom they called God. They walked with him in the garden of creation. They experienced his constant blessing. They knew how deeply they were interconnected with each other, being formed of the same elements as the earth itself, and animated by the energies of creation. They talked freely with God. Their dialogue was unbroken. There were no power cuts, because they lived and moved and had their being within the source of all power. Their centre of gravity was undivided. Their conscious and unconscious selves were one in that deep centre.

Until a new presence entwined itself into their hearts. An unseen voice. The voice of suggestion. The voice suggested this: 'You could be an island, with your own autonomy. There would be less for you to rule, but of that less, you would be the absolute ruler. In your own little world, you could be God. Your kingdom would be yours to control. You would be in charge of your own centre of gravity. If you pluck this suggestion down and take it into yourself, your whole view of the world, and your whole understanding of your place in it will change, and you will see that you, not God, are at the centre of your world.'

And they plucked the tempting fruit of this suggestion. And they took it in. Or rather, they were taken in by it. And the inner voice was right. Their entire view of creation changed. Their whole understanding of the world changed gear. They felt as if they were being raised to the level of God. But actually, they were being raised from the bedrock reality, to the shifting surface view of life. From then on, all they could see were the islands of each other. They forgot that once they had lived in the bedrock and known each other, and all creation, in its wholeness.

They rarely saw God after that, because their vision was focused on themselves. They rarely heard him, because their ears were tuned only to the narrow frequency of their own music. They thought he had banished them from the bedrock union. But in fact

they had banished themselves. *A barrier came down between all
living things and the source from which they sprang. It was like a
fiery, flashing sword, dividing them from themselves, dividing them
from the very ground of their being.*

*In the new kingdom of their ego-selves, they discovered they
had to fight for their survival. This wasn't surprising because, after
all, every living being had become its own island kingdom, and
every little kingdom had to struggle to keep itself alive and to guard
its boundaries against the demands of all the others. From then on,
two acorns falling from the same oak tree were in competition for
the same patch of earth. Two brothers born of the same parents were
in competition for the same piece of land. Conflict began. Violence,
suffering and death followed on its heels. God's Dream, which had
once been the Deep Dream of every living creature, had become
fragmented into a million little hopes and fears. God's Desire,
expressed in the original wholeness, had been broken into a million
little personalized wants and wishes.*

*Yet God kept on weaving his Dream. He made tunics of skins
for his fallen creation, to protect them from the worst effects of their
choices. Above all, he spread a shelter over them, called death, not
to punish them, but to ensure that their brokenness should not go
on for ever. And he kept on weaving…*

the INFINITE
KNOT

Weaving the story of life

The Celtic infinite knot is one picture of God's weaving. It takes us
to the first of the 'sacred spaces' of this pilgrimage. Perhaps this is
because it takes us back to a time before the fragmentation of
creation, and of ourselves, began. It speaks to us of the bedrock
union from which our own truest self springs and to which it longs
to return. It defies the fragmentation that divides us so destructively.

What is it about this symbol that has the power to
reconnect? Two things speak to me especially, but you will surely
discover its language in your own way.

- It reminds me that my little span of consciousness is just a
  tiny arc on the circumference of something infinite. It shows

me that my small piece of thread is just one snippet of an eternal spool with which God is weaving his Dream. Just one small snippet, but also a unique and essential snippet, without which the tapestry cannot become complete, or the Dream be dreamed into its fullness.

● It reveals the *spaces* between God's thread. These are the spaces of free will where I can make my own choices and where I can meet, or refuse to meet, with others in genuine self-disclosure and authentic fellow journeying. These are the spaces where warp and weft engage. They are invitations to be in relationship, and in community.

Frequently my life can feel like an impossible tangle, an insoluble problem. The infinite knot helps me to understand that it is in fact held in a perfect balance, which is beyond the grasp of my senses or my intellect, if only I could see it in its wholeness. The knot gives me that view of the wholeness, if only in symbolic form. It is up to me how I discover real ways, within my own experience, of translating that symbol into the kind of choices that can change my perspective and my way of being human.

When I look at the knot, I remember real situations in my life that feel like 'knots'. Difficult relationships, perhaps, or situations that keep going round in circles and not getting any further. Ever-recurring dilemmas. The sense of being 'hopelessly lost' in the maze of circumstance.

The infinite knot can lead me to a radical shift of perspective which makes me see these lesser knots differently. I am reminded over and over again:

● That I am only seeing a tiny segment of the whole knot;

● That my personal situations are intimately connected with the whole human situation;

● That there is something bigger than my limited view – something eternal – beyond all my concepts of time and space.

Let me introduce you to an imaginary friend of mine. I call him Nemo. He is like us in every way – he shares our intellect and our senses and he can process information and experience just as we can. But he only lives for a few hours, like an insect. Suppose Nemo's little lifespan were to occur during the daylight hours. He would experience the world as being light and warm and full of activity, populated by people and animals of all shapes and sizes. If, however, he lived his life out during the night, he would experience the world as dark and cold, and he would believe that the world is populated by cats, owls and teenagers, and that other species, if any others exist, are permanently asleep. Even if we grant Nemo a rather longer lifespan, a summer-born Nemo would describe the world as green and growing, and a winter Nemo would describe the same world as bleak and lifeless.

Nemo helps me to gain some perspective on what I regard as 'reality'. He makes it absolutely clear to me that my own grasp on reality is not much more reliable than his. I, too, live out my little lifespan on one tiny planet in one remote galaxy, for just a few short years, in one kind of culture, speaking just one native language, governed by one set of genes and circumstances, out of all the infinite possibilities. Yet on the basis of such scant data I presume to define 'reality'.

The knot puts right such misconceptions and helps us towards a humble awareness, both of the wonder and the limitations of our being.

A boat or an accident?

We don't need books of ancient wisdom to tell us that life is full of ups and downs. Sometimes we feel 'on top of the world'. Sometimes the world feels on top of us. When we are on a 'high', we feel we know where we are going. We have 'got it together'. When life is getting on top of us we feel as though we are underground, blind, without directions or any sense of perspective. If we translate these feelings into the language of weaving, we can see how these ups and downs, these overs and unders, work together, and are essential to the wholeness of our lives and the life of all creation. The dark underground bits are as vital as the light overland experiences. Yet, like Nemo, we are constantly tempted to stay with our own 'bit' and lose sight of the possibility of a greater 'whole'. Stuck with our own small knot, we feel trapped, if we are 'underneath', and maybe unwarrantedly self-sufficient if we are 'on top'. Our position at the time loads our entire perception of how things really are.

We are not alone with these feelings. Winnie-the-Pooh, a bear who is very partial to honey, confides to a friend one day, as he sails the pond astride an empty honey pot:

> *'I ought to say that it isn't just an ordinary sort of boat. Sometimes it's a Boat, and sometimes it's more of an Accident. It all depends.'*
> *'Depends on what?'*
> *'On whether I'm on top of it or underneath it.'*
> A.A. MILNE, *WINNIE-THE-POOH*

Weaving can only happen when two or more strands come together. It is a symbol of community. It needs the warp and the weft. There is no such thing as a one-strand cloth. Nor, as our Celtic forebears knew instinctively, is there any such thing as a solitary life pilgrimage, because we are one in the bedrock and the choices of each make a difference to all.

I remember, with a smile, an incident when my own daughter was very small. She must have done something she thought was wrong, and obviously didn't quite know how to get out of the dilemma of guilt in which she found herself. Children can be wonderfully transparent in these situations! A few days later we were out together, and she slipped off on her own into a shop and came out with a present for me, which she offered me with a heart-melting mixture of pride and humility that only children know how to produce. It was a little card, with a picture of a kitten with a woeful expression, standing beside an empty saucer, its paws bathed in a pool of spilled milk. The caption read, 'Please be patient. God hasn't finished with me yet!'

When I think back to that incident, and reread the card, which I have treasured ever since, I know that my little girl was in touch then with the wisdom of the infinite knot. She tried to tell me that whatever our minor altercation had been about, it was only a momentary flicker on the screen of eternity. She was saying, in her own way, that the situations, or feelings, in ourselves, which we believe to be final and definitive, are really only stages in a vast process of evolution in which we are all engaged. She had understood the picture of the kitten. And in her sad-yet-hopeful eyes I read her signal that she was challenging me to understand it too. God had woven a new and beautiful part of his Dream out of our broken pieces of thread.

The layers of being

One very reassuring, though challenging, aspect of the infinite knot is that it reveals something of the 'layers' of our being. As we contemplate the symbol of the knot, we can begin to notice the spiralling nature of our journey into the deepest centre of ourselves, and the intricate maze of exploration that draws us to the heart of the matter. It draws us into a centre where we rediscover our selves and we rediscover that union which was fragmented when we first followed the enticement of autonomy.

A spiralling journey takes us to ever-deepening layers of ourselves. It is never 'just the same thing over again', but rather the vision of recurrent experience, differently and more deeply known and recognized. We begin to notice the layers that have formed us into who we are. The layers of childhood, of play and of learning, the first layers of loving and of losing. Layers of growth, like the rings in a tree trunk, each successive layer marked by the weather of the time, rough or gentle. We may have lived in the same village all our lives, and with the same people, but each stage of our living and growing will have its own particular markings. When we stand at the sacred space of our personal reflection on that infinite knot, we may begin to glimpse the layering of our own story in the way that God sees it.

If you are artistically inclined, you may like to try drawing your own infinite knot. Express in your own way how your spirals have evolved, what your layers look like, and the special colours of the threads that have been woven into your life – the events and relationships, hopes, fears and dreams that have formed you. Or, if you prefer a more dynamic image, try looking at your life in terms of an intricate dance. What has moved you closer to the centre of yourself, what has whirled you out to the edges again? Who have been your closest dancing partners? How has your dance become interwoven with the dancing of those around you, or with the dance of all creation?

And for those who prefer a steady walk, how has your journey been? Where has the maze seemed dense, and where has the way opened up clearly before you? Round what twists and turns has your maze journey led you? Perhaps you can recall difficult times, when you may have felt you were walking further away from your true centre? Times when you seemed to fly on eagles' wings along a true course? However you felt at the time, all these periods of your life have actually been bringing you to the point where you stand today.

And what is this centre into which the infinite knots and spirals are drawing us? We might call it the deepest and truest centre of our selves, which we refer to as our 'heart', or our 'soul'. And we might equally well call it the heart of creation, where all is one in bedrock union. Searchers throughout human history have consistently reached the conclusion that these two centres are one. Paradoxically, where we are most 'alone', we come closest to the 'All-One'. The centre of our own hearts is a fragment of 'the heart of God'. It is the core of our being and the core of *all* being.

Choosing life

The story of Adam and Eve has a sequel. We left our archetypal ancestors in the state of separation from the wholeness of creation, brought about by their desire for personal autonomy. Yet God, we saw, did not stop weaving his Dream. His desire for a return to the original wholeness and blessing of creation is expressed, by the writer of Genesis, in the heart-warming vignette of God making tunics out of skins for these human souls, who would now be exposed to all the rigours of their freely elected 'island existence'.

When we pass from mythological time to historical time we can pick up this theme again. At the beginning of his gospel, Luke reports an awesome occurrence, some 2,000 years ago, in a little-known and ill-regarded small town called Nazareth. A village girl, still in her early teens, is going about her normal daily chores. Maybe she is dreaming of her future, because, as the records reveal, she is engaged to be married to a local carpenter. This is a retelling, in words she might have used herself, of what happened to her one morning:

It was a normal morning in every way, when quite suddenly the atmosphere changed. I felt as though I had been immersed in a warm pool of light. Time stood still, for I do not know how long. Nothing at all could have harmed me in that moment. Quite the opposite. I felt as though I was coming to life, really deeply and vibrantly. As though someone had ignited a beautiful candle deep inside me. For a moment I just let myself be enfolded in this amazing experience. I became aware of a bright presence beside me, and a clear but gentle voice, speaking to my heart. It felt as though my own being was in resonance with the being of all creation and the voice was the music of that resonance.

'I come to you in peace, Mary, and I bring you joy,' the angel said. 'The maker of all that is longs to be in perfect relationship with you and with all creation.'

I was deeply disturbed by this greeting, but the disturbance was like the stirring of depths of my being that no one had ever touched before. I didn't know how to respond. I was overawed.

'Don't be afraid, Mary,' the angel continued. 'God, our creator, grieves for his lost and lonely people. When Earth was new, and humankind first chose its own, lesser, way, he clothed you in your human bodies and gave you the Earth to tend. He never ceases from his care for you, nor sets aside the weaving of his Dream. Now he chooses you, and asks you this: "Will you weave a tunic for me? I need a tunic of humanness in which I can become one with my creation. Will you make that human body for my eternal presence? Will you accept the coming of the fullness of my love for all creation, and weave that love into a human form? Will you give birth to my love, so that all creation might be restored to wholeness?"'

I stood speechless before the mystery that the angel unfolded to me. He read my thoughts. 'Mary,' he said, 'when a human child is conceived, a new "island" comes into being in the ocean of life. But the child that you will conceive is a child of the bedrock oneness of creation, and he will draw all people home to wholeness. He will be conceived through the very energy of life itself. He will not be your child alone, but the child of all, and for all. When the Christ-child comes to birth in all creation, beginning with you, then the Father can lift the protecting veil of death from the face of his people and set them free for forever-ness.'

I knew that to deny this all-enfolding presence in which I was being held would be to deny my very self. To turn from this presence would be to turn away from my own deepest longings. I gazed into the light that held me, and I gave my consent to all that the angel had said.

The child who came into the world through this encounter was a point of intersection of time and eternity, visible and invisible. For Christians, he is the definitive point of intersection and the pivot point of the human story. In Celtic terms, he is the ultimate sacrament and sacred space, where visible and invisible, material and spiritual, element and energy, are fused into wholeness and where the infinite knot is rewoven from our tangled, broken strands.

From a young Nazarene girl, the child Jesus came to birth. But his name was also this – Alpha and Omega. Not only Jesus of Nazareth, but the cosmic Christ. Not only another human island, but the true self-expression of the deep bedrock of life and love. Not just another time-bound candle, but the eternal flame that burns in every living heart.

Alpha and Omega, the start and end of the infinite knot, which has no end. The paradox of God beyond time, clothed in our days and years; God beyond space, measured in feet and inches. God asks us to weave him a tunic of our own human being, so that he may become perpetually incarnate in his own creation, and transform that creation into his eternal Dream. He asks us. Not just Mary of Nazareth, but each of us. He asks us to give the broken threads of our own human experience, and weave them into a space for his Becoming. What happened to Mary is re-enacted, life after life, in those who have ears to hear and eyes to see. The infinite knot is ours to weave, for ourselves and for each other. When we choose, as Mary did, to consent to this calling, then the infinite knot is made a little more complete and a little more beautiful. When we choose to turn away from the call, the weaving of our wholeness is frustrated. In our 'Yes', we affirm our own deepest desiring. In our 'No', we frustrate what we most long for. We make our choices over and over, every day that we live. We cannot choose to be separate from the infinite knot. We can only choose whether or not we will be creatively engaged in its weaving.

Sometimes we seem to work in the light, and see clearly the pattern of life that we are weaving. Sometimes our thread goes underground, and we proceed on trust alone. Our living becomes a pattern of light and darkness, space and density, knowing and unknowing, above and below, trusting and doubting. And nothing is excluded. Every strand, whatever we may think of it, is being woven into the wholeness.

Silently, invisibly, God weaves his tunic from the living

fibres of our lives, and when the tunic of incarnation is complete, we will see that the whole of creation is enfolded in it. It will become the baptismal cloth in which all our island isolation will be plunged into the ocean of his love, there to discover that in the bedrock we are One.

Beginnings…

Before we leave this first station of our journey, we might pause to reflect on our own beginnings. Each of us began our human journey when two other human cells came together, as it were, to weave a new knot in the fabric of life. Two cells, each holding only half of our story. From the very beginning we were fashioned out of togetherness, the result of a moment of communion. The psalmist expresses this beginning in these words:

> It was you who created my inmost self,
> and put me together in my mother's womb…
> You know me through and through,
> From having watched my bones take shape,
> When I was being formed in secret,
> Knitted together in the limbo of the womb.
>
> PSALM 139:13–15

None of us can go back, even in imagination, to that time when our personal human existence was being woven from those first two cells into the amazing complexity and mystery of our bodies and minds. However, we all know how we feel when circumstances shake our certainties and we feel like curling up again in the foetal position to get ourselves put back together again.

Next time you feel like this, you might like to try going to your personal 'sacred space', letting yourself simply become aware of the weaving process that never ceases in you. Remember any period in your life, or place you have known, in which you felt safe, and 'at home'. When you feel comfortable in your safe space, try to bring to mind some of the main strands of your life: your childhood, your schooldays, your most important relationships; your work and your play; the things that have evoked fear in you and those that have inspired trust; the times of pain and the times of joy. The weaving has been going on in all of these things, day by day, hour by hour, silently and surely.

And it still continues. Every day we live is a further weaving of God's Dream in our own lives. Every incident in our daily lives, every meeting with each other, every conversation or unseen act of kindness, everything we think or feel, is being woven into that Dream. Perhaps it is like the weaving of a cocoon or a chrysalis. It may look and feel like nothing more exciting than a lifeless brown lump hanging on a winter branch, going nowhere, doing nothing. But in reality it is nurturing the butterfly of our eternal selves and the promise of the kingdom of

God that is still beyond our wildest imaginings, yet is also gestating silently in the depths of our own hearts.

Baptism into wholeness

The children we once were knew moments of mystery. Creation was still an untold story then, pregnant with possibility and radiant with wondrous discovery. Sometimes this sense of wonder is rekindled, as life moves on. From time to time we experience a sense of being in touch with the 'bedrock' union below the tideline of our everyday 'island' existence. We could express this in terms of being plunged into a layer of being which is much deeper than that of our normal conscious experience, there to become aware of a heightened sense of union or empathy with others, or with the whole of creation.

Christians express this fundamental desire to enter into a living and cooperating relationship with the whole of creation, and with its creator, in the sacrament of baptism. In this sacrament we acknowledge the incompleteness and potential or actual harmfulness of our 'island' living and we surrender ourselves in trust to the waters that will lead us to the bedrock wholeness and 'All-Oneness'.

You might like to reflect on your own feelings about this fundamental desire, and how you have expressed it, or might wish to express it sacramentally in your own way.

One way of celebrating this sacrament at a personal level might be to call to mind a memory of a time and a place where you felt, however momentarily, that you were in touch with something deeper than your own 'island' world. Let that memory become a sacred space for you, and return to it deliberately from time to time. Just be still in that memory, and let yourself become aware again of the present moment. You may feel that, amid the chaos of contemporary life, it is merely an illusion to seek peace, and a deeper wisdom, by immersing oneself in an invisible, intangible 'bedrock'. Yet how often do we respond to a moment of crisis or the demand for a snap decision with words like, 'Let me sleep on it,' or, 'Just take a deep breath and count to ten'? This kind of folk wisdom is surely coming from the bedrock. It is saying in everyday language what the mystics have spoken in riddles through the centuries. There is a depth in which we come closer to who we really are, and that depth can be reached when we take time for stillness and awareness.

You might like to take leave of this first station on our Celtic Way by spending a while in your sacred space, and letting its circles enfold you in whatever ways suggest themselves.

the INFINITE
KNOT

CHAPTER 2

THE
HIGH CROSS

TOUCHSTONES OF ETERNITY

*I*n Celtic times the standing stones and high crosses, such as the one in the picture below, were the village's library, its pulpit and its art gallery, just as they were the sentinels of the high places, watching over the community, focusing the people's gaze always to something beyond themselves. They stood like books for all to read in village squares, and rose like eternal bookmarks on the hilltops, to remind all travellers that their own small journeys were a part of the eternal journey of the whole human family.

They rose like compass needles, guiding people to listen to the core of their being, and to live true to what they heard there. The ground on which they stood was acknowledged by the entire community as sacred space. They belonged to all. They represented the wholeness, and the heaven-directedness, of the people.

Can they have any meaning for us today? We, who can access the worldwide web of global information at the touch of a key, hardly need to read our stories engraved on a piece of stone. Or do we?

The listening stone

From time to time you have probably commented, maybe about some landscape, or a house or a tree, 'If this place could talk, what stories it would tell.'

But before the stones can tell their stories, they first have to watch, and to listen…

I was delighted, one morning, to come across a little-known incident in the life of a man called Joshua (narrated in the book of Joshua, chapter 24). Joshua was Moses' choice to be his successor. He was to be the man to lead the people across the boundaries of their dreaming, and into the Promised Land. Joshua seems to have moved like a new broom, after Moses' death high on the hills overlooking the Promised Land. He gives the people a bit of a pep talk, reminding them of their own long and chequered story – of their searching for their own identity, for a meaning in their history, for the bonding in love that would turn them from wandering individuals into a purposeful community. He reminds them of their blessed escapes, from slavery in Egypt, and from pursuit by their frustrated ex-captors. Then he challenges them with words like these:

'Now I have reminded you of everything that has happened in your story so far. It has been a hard road, and you have often stumbled. You have made some pretty spectacular mistakes, but you have always found your way again eventually. It seems as though some deep inner compass was always guiding you, out of the destructive places and towards the places of life. In the light of all of this blessing, what are you going to choose now? Will you follow that compass in your hearts and trust its guiding for the future? Or are you going to go your own ways, and fall back into your former fragmentation?'

There is a thoughtful silence, followed by an overwhelming affirmation of their collective trust in the inner compass who has guided them this far, and whom they know as God. 'We will trust, and follow,' they say. 'We will turn aside from all the lesser paths along the way and we will refuse to be lured into the cul-de-sacs of our own making.'

Joshua recognizes this moment of commitment as a sacred space in his people's story. This is how he marks the sacredness of that moment:

That day Joshua made a solemn covenant for the people. He wrote down the promises that had been exchanged between the people and their God, and they wrote their promise within their own hearts. The same Word of Promise was written, that day, in the heart of God and in the hearts of his people, to travel together in trust from that day forward.

Then Joshua took a great stone and set it up there, under the oak, in the place that all acknowledged as their holy place, and he said, 'See! This stone is a witness of the Promise that has been sealed this day. It has heard the Word of God spoken throughout our history, and has recorded it, lest we forget. And it has listened to your own promise, to walk for ever true to the inner compass within your heart. This stone is saturated with the truth of our story, which it has absorbed through all our years. It shall be a stone of strength for you as you walk the way of your own truth. It will stand witness against you if you deny that truth and choose the lesser ways.'

Then Joshua sent his people on their way, and they all returned to their own place, with the covenant engraved on their hearts.

Joshua's stone has its counterparts all over the Celtic lands. They stand to remind us of our story, and to gather us together into community. Where they stand is sacred space, where we recognize our oneness with each other and with our first source in God. They remind us of the steady compass in our hearts that guides us on. We may call it conscience. We may call it love. No name can hold the fullness of its truth. But if we turn our backs on it and choose our self-made courses, the stone will stand silent witness to our desertion of ourselves.

Most of us have no high cross or standing stone in our village square, but we all have one in our hearts and in our memories. We all have a deep, if buried, sense of when we are 'living true' and when we are letting ourselves, and others, down. We have a core of truth within us that is saturated in our story, and has listened to all our pain and joys.

What story would your stone tell if it could speak? Find a quiet place, where you can be still and alone in your 'safe space', and listen to what it has to say. Let it replay the story of your life, and reflect back to you the times of grief, the times of joy. The times when you have been true to yourself. The times when you have strayed from your inner sense of what is true for you. Celebrate your story's holiness in your own way. Tune in to its guiding power.

The Celtic high crosses tell the story of humankind – our creation, the loss of our sense of interconnectedness, our search for wholeness and our ultimate destination in a life where all shall be one. The story is told in pictures. It challenges us to connect our own life's pictures with the shared story of all human community. It calls us to gather round the flame flickering in the heart of ourselves and to let ourselves hear our story, as once we gathered round the fireside of our childhood home to listen to the ageless stories of humanity. It is a call to dream again. Not just the fragmented dreams of overtired minds, but the deep dream of who we really are.

The ladder of reconnection

Let us join another dreamer, whose story is engraved on the ancient stones. His name is Jacob. He is on a journey from Beersheba to Haran in the barren wilderness of the Negev desert lands. Night falls, and Jacob is exhausted. This is a retelling of the story of Jacob's dream. The original version is told in the book of Genesis (chapter 28):

The sun had set, and Jacob stopped to find a place to sleep. The ground was not very inviting, so he lay down where he could find a place, and took a stone for his pillow. He had a dream. He dreamed there was a ladder that began on the ground right there where he was lying, and stretched all the way up to heaven. Angels were going up and down the ladder all the time. Then God was standing next to him, talking to him in his dream. 'I am the God of your whole story and your people's story,' God told him. 'I am giving you this ground you are lying on. It's yours now. It is the space where your story shall be told and the story of all the human family. This is the earth of your own experience. It is the infinity of all human experience, from north to south, from east to west, through all time, for as long as human life shall last on Earth. You can be sure that in every part of this experience I am with you. Wherever you travel I will keep you in my care, and at the end of all your travelling I will bring you safely back to your truest self and your eternal home. I will never be apart from you, ever. You have my promise.'

Jacob woke up with a start, and exclaimed, 'Truly, God is here, and I never realized! This little patch of stony ground is a place of wonder, where I have felt the presence of God! This little corner of Earth is nothing less than the dwelling place of God and the gateway to heaven!'

The next morning, overwhelmed by the deep truth his dream had opened up in him, Jacob took the piece of stone he had been using as a pillow and placed it upright as a marker for all other

travellers. He poured oil over it, as if to anoint it. He declared it to be a sacred space.

It would perhaps be no exaggeration to say that Jacob's stone was one of the first 'high crosses'. It marked a place where a human being had been flooded with the presence of God, and it became, from then on, a stone with a story. All travellers, thenceforth, would be able to read that story and, perhaps, stand still in a moment of awe and think to themselves, 'Yes, I remember moments in my life when time has stood still like that. I can read something of my story in this story.'

I love this story of Jacob's dream, because it evokes personal memories in me and connects them to the memory of all humankind. I, too, have sometimes journeyed through a long hard period in my life and almost given up, exhausted with the effort of trying to make things work or to solve some problem or other. Night has fallen. I have felt myself to be totally 'in the dark'. I have curled up on the stones of my troubled thoughts and fallen asleep. Then, out of the blue, something may have happened to turn the tide in my heart. Perhaps someone has broken through the blanket of despair with a word of hope. Perhaps I have opened my eyes to see a new dawn, hear a new birdsong, feel the touch of someone who cares. These have been my 'angels', and they have drawn my gaze up and away from the stones of my immediate experience, to the heights above me and the infinity of creation all around me. They have placed my feet upon the ladder of transformation, and I have sensed the sacredness of that moment.

Then the stone that was such a burden to me, and such a source of pain, has become a sacred space. I have realized that my life is no longer one-dimensional, and that the stones are not the whole story. My focus has shifted. My perspective has been radically broadened. 'Truly,' I have thought to myself, 'there is a sacred presence right here in the everyday path I am walking, however stony it feels beneath my feet. The stony ground is no longer a hardship to be lived through and endured. It is the very place where the ladder begins! It is the gateway to a whole new way of being human. My earthed experience is intimately connected to my longings for all that is beyond my experience. Earth and heaven have embraced in this place, and I am their child, the fruit of their union. I can be no other. I need be no other than who I am.'

Forever moments

This may all sound fine on paper, but how do we translate it into real life? To realize we are the product of both heaven and Earth is nothing but hollow rhetoric if it does not lead us closer to the heart of ourselves and of each other, and into a greater awareness of the wonder of our own being and of all creation.

To make this reconnection, it may be helpful to go back to childhood memories. Children, however brutal they can sometimes be to each other, have a particular gift which we lose almost entirely as we grow older. This is the gift of living life in the present moment. A child at play is utterly unconcerned by the time schedules and urgencies of her parents. By the same token, a child sitting at his school desk thinks the class will never end. Every moment is a forever moment, for good or ill.

You might just like to take a few minutes to reflect back over your earlier years. Can you remember any 'forever moments'. It may take a little time, so be gentle with yourself, and patient. Above all, give yourself the gift of stillness, both outside and in. Find a quiet corner where you can be undisturbed for a time, and just relax. Notice any memories that rise up in your mind. In your imagination go back to places where you once experienced a flash of joy. Let your senses join with your memory in this exercise. Perhaps there is a particular taste or fragrance or sound that has the ability to evoke a memory in you. A fragment of an old song, occasionally reheard? The scent of pine, evoking long-ago Christmases?

I remember, for example, a night when I was seven, and was suddenly and totally transfixed by the starry sky. Every star was like a living being to me, and I felt I could have reached out to touch them. I felt enveloped in the vastness and the glory of it all, strangely alone, yet held within it all, as part of it. I would not, of course, have been able to express my feelings in this way at the time, yet that memory has never left me. It returns in full power every time I look up on a starry night. I know, beyond any doubt, that it was one of my earliest forever moments. I know it as certainly as Jacob knew that he had slept at the gateway to heaven. Since that night, every star-filled night has become, for me, a personal sacred space.

A few years later I spent a 'forever afternoon' on a rare hot day in August on my uncle's farm in Lincolnshire. The grown-ups were in conclave in the farmhouse, putting the world to rights, and I slipped off into the sunshine, found a ladder and climbed up to the top of a haystack. I can still feel the prickling of the hay stalks, still see the yellow-brown world in which I had made my nest, and the brilliant blue of the sky above me, with its occasional cotton-wool clouds. I can still smell the scent of the newly cut hay, still feel the rough rungs of the ladder against my skin. I can still hear the profound silence of the afternoon.

These memories are actually little power packs of energy that we carry around with us. The psychologists tell us that our feelings are the source of our energy. Moments like these, which we cherish in memory, are saturated with the feelings of that moment. When we draw on them, by remembering them, we draw on this concentrated energy. It gives us life. We feel energized by the memory, and better able to say with Jacob, 'This was a moment of eternity, and I never knew!' Fortunately, moments of eternity don't go off. They never get stale. They are for ever there, waiting for us to remember and be recharged by them. Take hold of them and claim their power. They are a gift no one can ever take from you. They are 'high crosses' in your heart.

Tragically, for some people, memories of childhood are racked with pain. If this is so for you, you may find that the search for sacred spaces will be so much harder, but for you, as for Jacob, it may reveal diamonds among the stones.

Timeless moments are not just for children. They are like a centre of wholeness and completeness that we easily reach when we are young and unburdened by the demands of a timetabled world, and find much more elusive as we get older and more 'busy'. I once had the privilege of being beside an elderly lady as she experienced a totally unexpected 'forever moment', which I believe changed the course of her life, or at least her way of looking at life.

Elsa was visiting Britain from her home in the former East Germany. She had never been beyond the borders of her own country, and had spent all her life in a totalitarian system. This was her first journey abroad. She was seeing everything with a child's eyes, as if for the very first time. One day we took her to the Welsh coast. She chattered incessantly as we drove through North Wales, and seemed to be enjoying the day well enough. But when we reached the coast, and walked along the beach, she fell silent. She seemed to forget that anybody was there with her. She moved into a world of her own, just as Jacob entered into his dream. She stood at the water's edge and gazed out to sea. After a while I moved a little closer to her, taking care not to break in to her silence. Finally, she drew a deep breath and whispered – perhaps to herself, or perhaps to the universe spread out before her – 'So vast, so vast, and I am so small.'

Elsa was over seventy when she first saw the sea. But in that moment she was seven again and all of creation was still an untold story. And she was as amazed as Jacob when she realized that she had stumbled upon the gates of heaven. It was a moment worthy of a standing stone, to mark the sacred space she had entered.

Look back over your forever moments, and celebrate the stones you have inwardly erected to mark these sacred spaces in your life, where you have touched the gates of eternity. Such memories mark the dawning of a sense of wonder at our own being and at the 'otherness' of every other form of being. They hold the energy that will fuel our life's exploration of the world and of our own place within it.

The broken arc

The surprises of life come in many different guises. How easy to miss them completely, especially if we have preconceived ideas about how they are supposed to happen.

One of my life's happy surprises burst in upon me during a holiday in the Cognac area of France one summer. We were staying in a *gîte* – bed and breakfast in a rambling, yet elegant, farmhouse that had been a minor chateau, and still thrived on the surrounding vineyards. It had its own cellars, producing the house *pineau* – a blend of cognac and unfermented grape juice and the favourite aperitif of the region. We were the only English speakers in the house that day. It was late and we were just enjoying a sumptuous supper with the other guests round the vast kitchen table, when there was a bustle at the door, and a lively family from Ireland arrived.

I little guessed that evening, as the five of them – parents and three children – erupted into the French farmhouse kitchen like a minor volcano, what surprises they carried with them. Their sudden presence was a shaft of 'something else' breaking through the steady holiday routine we had all established for ourselves. To call the event a breath of fresh air would be an understatement. The newcomers were duly welcomed, and were soon sitting with us at the table, tucking in to *moules marinières* and fine French wine.

It was the start of a friendship which I cherish still. The next day we had plenty of time to get to know each other better. As the afternoon sun reached the peak of its warmth, I sat out on the chateau wall with the mother of the flock (let us call her Sinead), gazing out over the sunflower fields and the gently undulating vineyards. She turned to me, and admired the Celtic cross I was wearing round my neck. I found myself, unaccountably, telling her how much it actually meant to me.

Sinead listened, quietly, as I told her how it reminds me of my origins, both natural and spiritual, and that I feel somehow at home with it. How I feel it connects my story with the story of creation. How the cross intersects the circle of my life, and, even more importantly, my feeling for how the cross intersects, and holds in being, the reality of all creation, and how that symbolism makes connections I need to be reminded of day by day, minute by minute. They are the connections of integrity and wholeness, and my cross expresses my deep longings for those connections.

As she listened, I began to sense the undercurrents of her own yearning for connectedness coming across and meeting mine. Then she went on to tell me an old folk legend. Like all good legends, it has the quality of a parable:

A man lived in an old stone cottage that was badly in need of repair. He made do, day by day, and got on with his life, struggling to wrench a living from the meagre land. But eventually the rain that leaked in on him got too heavy and the wind around his ears got too cold. He had to do something about the gap in his wall.

Up on the hillside there stood an ancient stone Celtic cross. It had stood there since time immemorial. It was silent and uncomplaining in the Atlantic gales that swept over it, but its very silence said something about continuity, community and interrelatedness. It had become part of the local imagination and, without ever really thinking about it, the people knew, with a sound instinct, that it was important. It had something to say about what they hoped to be. Something to do with the coming of the kingdom.

The cottager went up to the cross one dark night. One of those stone arcs, he thought, would exactly fit the hole in his wall. He would come the next day with a hammer and chisel and chip it away. He smiled, perhaps uneasily, as he thought of how much warmer his home would be without the perpetual draughts. Almost satisfied with his decision, he turned back towards his homeward path, but his plans were rudely interrupted. In the distance he clearly saw flames rising from his cottage. Panic-stricken he ran home across the rough fields. But, when he arrived, his home was still standing as he had left it. The only fire had been in his imagination.

Common sense reasserted itself, and a few days later he set off up the hill again with his hammer and chisel. It was dark, but he looked around warily, lest anyone else should see him there. It was only a piece of stone, after all, and he needed it. He started to chip. *The sound of his hammer against the solid head of the chisel rang out through the night like the tolling of a bell, to alarm the very heavens. But he carried on chipping, until he remembered the strange events of his previous attempt and looked over his shoulder nervously in the direction of his cottage. And there, on the distant skyline, a fire raged. And again he ran home in terror. And again he found his cottage unharmed, just as he had left it.*

More cold, damp nights came and went. Sleep came uneasily. The bizarre images of dream and nightmare entangled themselves among the pressing urgencies of everyday. The fierce winds from the sea were stronger by far than the breezes that

fluttered through his unease. He made up his mind that the very next day his cottage would be sound again and that no irrational fears would deflect him from his purpose.

He walked up the hill, without looking to right or left. He worked quickly and efficiently. He closed the doors of his mind firmly against any distraction, real or imagined. Soon the stone arc was in his sack. This time there were no flames on the horizon and no flash of panic disturbed him. He turned his back on the mutilated cross and walked home steadily, through the quiet of the night. And when he got home, the cottage was a heap of smouldering ashes.

A delightful piece of Celtic folklore. But my friend's story has never left me. I look at my Celtic cross with new insight now. It speaks to me of the many times I have chipped my bit out of its perfect circle, meeting my own personal needs, or wants, at the expense of those of the whole human family. It reminds me that every time I break the circle of my own integrity, I somehow damage the wholeness of all creation. It warns me that just the tiniest gap in a circle breaks the whole continuity of things. The sense of brokenness we feel in ourselves and in our world cannot be contained in isolation. It is a community matter. A virus far beyond our understanding and way out of our control.

When we turn aside from the course our inner compass knows to be the true course of our hearts, then the stones bear witness against us.

The story reminds us that those warning signs and voices which speak their message clearly enough when we are still in temptation, become inaudible at the point when we actually commit ourselves to the breaking of the arc. We need to hear those warnings, see the potential of the blazing house and take heed. When we become sufficiently desensitized that we can make the break in the circle, then we will not be able to hear or see the warnings any more. It will be too late. We will have chosen our own way of partialness instead of God's way to wholeness. The circle of continuity may be the world, the whole human family, our personal circles, or the wholeness of ourselves. It is the circle of integrity and it leaves us with the ever-recurring decision, either to take the part that we want or to remain with the wholeness that we need.

I know I have often chosen to seize my 'part' of creation's perfect circle. I have silenced the whispers of unease inside me, and walked on wilfully, wearing the blinkers of my immediate need. And, sooner or later, I have found myself standing in front of the smouldering remains of who I thought I was, and I have been paralysed by the helplessness of it all.

Yet those very same experiences also open up new possibilities inside us. Deep inside the rings of our fears and our tears, our need and our greed, there can be another, very different kind of empty space. It need not be just the gap we leave behind when we break the wholeness of our circles. It can become a place where we are challenged to move towards a deeper form of wholeness.

In the summer of 1999, British TV viewers tuned in one evening to the sight of the liberation of 800 cats and kittens from a farm that had been breeding them for the sole purpose of medical research. It was the last farm of its kind in Britain, and the farmer was retiring, after enduring years of abuse from animal-rights campaigners. The cameras showed a road near the farm. On one side of the road were the crowds of animal-rights activists, jubilant that they had hastened the closure of the farm. On the other side were the farmer and a friend of his. The farmer seemed utterly weary of the combat. His friend shouted angry rebukes at the activists, reminding them that we all want medical research to make progress. The road marked the front line of confrontation between the two 'sides'.

As I watched this scene I thought of the perfect circle into which all creation is woven. I reflected on how easy it is to 'break off our bit of the arc', and even to think we are doing the right thing when we do so. In this case the human race, represented by the medical researchers who bought the cats for experimentation, and the farmer who bred them for this sole purpose, was saying, 'We want whatever it takes to ensure optimum health for our human race.' The animals, represented by the activists, were saying, 'We are part of creation too. We do not want this slow and painful death.' It was an intractable 'either/or' situation. The Celtic spirit, at its best, would say, 'Not 'either/or', but 'both–and'. The answer cannot lie in satisfying the needs and desires of any one part of creation, at the expense of another. When that happens there is always a price to pay, and the integrity of creation is sabotaged. The only answer worthy of a humanity that holds the seeds of God in its heart must be one which honours the needs of all creation.

Our reactions, when we see news items like this, show

clearly that we are still able to hear the warning signs. Let us not drift into the stage where we become so desensitized that we risk arriving home one day to find our home, our Earth, finally destroyed.

Confrontation, though painful, can be the catalyst that wakes us up to the need to become free of the 'either/or' mentality, and to look for ways along the 'both–and' route. This awakening often begins at home. Take a look at your own domestic confrontations and ask yourself, 'Am I looking for a solution that will satisfy only one side of the conflict? Could I change gear enough to look for a solution that might honour the needs of all sides?'

The perfect circle has no sides!

The singing stones

Every situation in our lives has a 'high cross' somewhere within it. Day after day, over and over, we find ourselves sensing that unease inside which warns us we are not living true to the core of our being. But just as certainly, day by day we will find, if we keep our eyes open, the traces of 'forever moments'. The stones will sing a song of joy, when joy is what they have witnessed, and nothing can silence them. Listen to the song of the stones of Jerusalem, as a different crowd of people, descendants of Joshua's flock, surges into the city, full of hope for a new kind of deliverance. The scene described here is first reported by Luke in his gospel (chapter 19). It is the day we call 'Palm Sunday'. Jesus is riding towards Jerusalem, and into all the events that will lead to Good Friday and to Easter:

It was a warm morning. The sun had risen over the small villages of Bethphage and Bethany, a few miles from Jerusalem, and there was no reason to expect surprises. Yet there was an atmosphere of tension in the air too. A man, Jesus, and his friends were passing through. They had often stayed there in the past. It was a place where they clearly felt at home and safe, and now they had to move on, into a future that seemed full of threat. It was quite a trek from

there into the city, and Jesus sent two of his friends across the road
to find a young colt, not yet broken in. They were to untie this colt
and bring it to him. If anyone challenged them, they were to say,
'The Master needs it.'

They did as he asked them, and threw their cloaks across
the colt's back, for Jesus to sit on. Then the little scene turned into
something of a celebratory procession. The sight of the colt, and Jesus
on its back, attracted a large crowd of people. Many of them had
known Jesus' healing touch on their sick bodies, or his calming
influence on their troubled minds. Others had sat at the lakeside,
or climbed the hills, to listen to his quiet wisdom. Some had seen
miracles happening at his bidding. None of them could understand
the mystery this man embodied. But they knew its effects, and they
had something to shout about. So they shouted, and sang out their
thankfulness. It turned into a standing ovation. 'Blessings upon you,'
they cried. 'You bring the things of heaven to our earthbound lives.'

The acclamation was not universal, however. Inevitably there
were undercurrents of disgruntlement. The disapprovers muttered to
the man on the colt, 'Can't you keep the crowds quiet? Call them to
order!' And he turned to them, and said,

'I tell you, if these people are silenced, the stones themselves
will cry out.'

And so the listening stones can become the singing stones
of our lives. Sacred space is space in which intense emotion has
been experienced, and the place itself, the very stones of the
ground, seems to be charged with the memory of this emotion.
Memories, indeed, are battery packs of stored emotional energy.
Our personal stones and crosses can release this energy:

- They can help us to discharge the negative energy of bad
  memories and let it be opened up into new and healing
  perspectives;

- They can help us to celebrate the positive energy of good and
  joy-filled memories, and turn it into fuel for the future journey.

Can you recall some of your own 'singing stones'? They might be memories of times when you have experienced intense joy, or a new surge of hope in a dark situation. Perhaps you can remember deep sighs of relief, and 'letting go', when a burden was lifted from you. Try bringing to mind the place where these events happened. In your imagination, let that place retell to you that part of your story and let that joy fill you with new energy for the way ahead.

And the weeping stones

For the man on the colt, the singing stones were about to change their tune, as Palm Sunday passed into Good Friday. Joy and celebration can turn all too quickly into grief and heartbreak, as we all know from our own experience. Like the infinite knot, our lives weave in and out of the darkness and light of the human condition. Sometimes the stones must weep. Places where deep feeling has been lived through become sacred space in the Celtic experience, and so do places of passage. My own mother's death has become sacred space for me for both these reasons. This is how I remember it, and let its pain become something new:

Outside the window there was bright sunshine. A short summer heatwave. The garden beckoned. I couldn't resist its invitation to find a few moments of healing peace beneath the trees. The final vigil, as she fought her losing battle with cancer, had lasted for three weeks. After watching with her each night, I would listen for the first single bird call before the dawn chorus proper began and my heart would lift a little with the first flush of sunrise over the garden. She usually slept fitfully in those dawn hours, and as soon as the garden was sunlit, I used to go out for half an hour among the roses. Those were magical, mystical times. I became keenly aware of how close I was to the centre of myself, and of my dying mother, and of God himself. The boundaries between us were dissolving.

Those times became times of prayer, without my realizing it. The garden became a space where I could release all my conflicting feelings, and then, when it didn't make sense any more, simply rest in the silence. Can a silence be pregnant with death? The fact of impending death was a rebuke to the vitality of the garden, or was it the other way round? Yet the silence seemed to be permitting the dying – even acting as a midwife to it.

She died at dawn. It had to be like that. Afterwards I spent one more quiet period in the garden where I had grown up. I went back one last time to the wild rose bush beneath which I had so often done my homework. I said goodbye to my father's gladioli and Michaelmas daisies, the old bonfire site and those rose bushes we had all loved, once, an eternity ago.

I didn't cry then. It was a moment too deep for tears. I went back for a few timeless minutes to my childhood there in that garden. And then my thoughts were joined by the laughter of real children, playing in the neighbouring garden. There, on the boundary between beginnings and endings, I quite deliberately bequeathed my past to their future. In my heart I passed over to them that beloved emotional space, which I had now outgrown. Although nothing was spoken, and they scarcely knew I was standing there, they were enriched by the moment, somewhere deep in the heart of things. And I, remembering with love, was somehow freed, and content to let the past flow into the future, its pain transformed into something beautiful and alive.

Weeping stones can become places of resurrection.

Seasons of covenant

Adolescence is a time in our lives when searching is high on the agenda. Like the Celtic cross we are reaching for the stars, and in the process we so often come close to breaking ourselves, and others, pushing ourselves beyond the limits, testing and stretching the boundaries. Without the adolescent inside us, to push us further and challenge us to take the risks, we would be dull creatures indeed, and the evolutionary thrust would atrophy in our human race.

In the searching years, too, we are looking, perhaps unconsciously, for the inner compass that will enable us to find our own course in life and then to sail true to that course when the winds are against us. These are the seasons of our lives when we may feel most powerfully the desire to commit ourselves to the highest ideals, and we may come down very hard on ourselves when we sense we have failed to live true to these ideals.

Whether we realize it or not, and whether or not we would use this kind of language, these are seasons of *covenant* – our personal covenant with Life. In our experience of 'forever moments' we have glimpsed something of the scale and the nature of the Beyond that is calling us, and we are learning to read our own story in the landscape of our lives.

And, of course, like the weaving in the womb, the striving of the search is not just a stage we go through, but a repeating, evolving pattern, recurring as our hearts grow and ripen, for as long as there is a horizon on our skyline.

The anointing of commitment

For Joshua and his people, the stone he erected was a symbol of covenant. Our Celtic forebears also saw their high crosses as signs and sacraments of the covenant between God, themselves and creation.

Something is asked of us, whenever we stand at the intersection of time and eternity, just as it was asked of Jacob.

How do you feel about the standing stones and the high crosses of *your* life? Remember, for a moment, in the quiet of your heart, the special times and places where you have known you were in contact with 'touchstones of eternity', whatever form these have taken for you. Let your touchstones reconnect you to that inner certainty which assures you that you are choosing and acting in accordance with the deepest part of yourself, and warns you when you are not living true to yourself.

At the station of the high cross, we come to the second stage of our pilgrimage through life. This is a place to reflect on our times of making a commitment to our onward journey, in specific ways. Times for choosing whether to follow the compass at the core of our being, or let ourselves be led by lesser lights. These covenant times can happen over and over again, of course, for our pilgrimage, too, is a spiralling circle.

One way of celebrating this station of our pilgrimage is in the Christian sacrament of confirmation, in which the candidate desiring to make a personal commitment to the Way of Christ is anointed, to mark the sacredness of the covenant promises being witnessed.

You might like to recall any acts of commitment, whether public or private, you have made, or perhaps feel you would like to make, to affirm your desire to follow your own deepest truth. How might you wish to mark this act of commitment? Is there anyone you would like to share it with?

the
high cross

hillтops

SUMMITS OF VISION

W hat is it that draws us to the tops of hills and mountains? How can we explain that special thrill of touching the stones of the summit cairn? Whether our aspirations roam the Alps or Himalayas, or are content merely with the humble hillsides of our neighbourhood, there is something powerfully attractive about the top of a hill. Not surprisingly, hilltops are significant landmarks in our human search to connect to the divine.

I have spent many weeks of my life walking the hills of my homeland. When I reflect on these wanderings, I see, in my mind's eye, apparently interminable strings of summits, linked by ridges and plateaux, and separated by valleys and clefts. Whenever a summit is reached, there always seems to be another, higher one, just out of reach, demanding another burst of energy to reach it.

And this is a helpful picture, too, of how our 'spiritual journey' often looks. There are moments of vision, making all the climbing worthwhile, but wherever we stand still to take stock, there is always something more beyond our range, drawing us onward, attracting us in spite of the rocky journey that seems to separate us from our hearts' desire.

So many stories from ancient spiritual writings and traditions, including those of Celtic times, speak of hilltops as sacred space. Hilltops are as close as we get to heaven, perhaps, and a potent reminder of our deep longings to reach out towards what is utterly beyond ourselves. They also afford a view – a fresh perspective of the land from which we have come – and new insights into the journey that still lies ahead.

Do they mean anything for us today, in a generation that has flown the oceans and continents in jet aircraft, and viewed the Earth from the moon?

Soul seasons

A friend once spoke to me of what we might call the 'seasons of the heart'. He pointed out to me that very often the course of an individual's life reveals a number of cycles, commonly lasting for around seven years. The number seven seems to have a special significance for the human psyche. For Jews and Christians the seventh day is a day of rest, and the seventh year is to be a year of rest for the soil. Even now, in a world where the Sabbath peace is lost in the clatter of supermarket tills, and the sabbatical year's rest and renewal is granted only to a very fortunate minority, we might still be able to detect the effects of the 'seven times table' in our lives.

Indeed the whole biblical sense of the 'sabbatical', defining seven-year seasons that apply to the land, to the individual, to the law and to the whole community, points to the same deep human instinct of a cyclic energy flow. Even our body's cell structure, we are told, is completely renewed over seven years, leaving no cell as it was. Everything about us is being continually renewed and remade.

These thoughts led me to ponder the nature of the 'seven-year cycles' in my own life, and I found it helpful to picture each such cycle as a 'hill' in my inner landscape. This chapter is an opportunity for you to walk the range of hills that your own life has set before you, and notice what they reveal of your journey so far, and what vision they open up for the years to come.

Noticing your 'sevens'

There is, of course, nothing fixed about the number 'seven'. When we look at the phases of our lives, we may often find that they tend to show up a pattern of periods of *around* seven years – sometimes only four or five, sometimes as many as ten or so. The precise mathematics doesn't matter. What matters is that these phases, or cycles, are *there*, however long they seem to have lasted. If hilltops represent sacred space, then getting in touch with our personal life hilltops might be one way to touch the transcendent within us.

These natural cycles, though not rigidly fixed to a certain number of years, are nonetheless quite definite phases which we cannot see when we are living in them, but can observe quite easily with hindsight. And they seem always to begin with what might be called a *life-giving moment.*

We can all begin our stories with the same 'life-giving moment'. Whatever the pattern of our subsequent lives, however unwelcoming the circumstances of our birth, we all came into existence as a result, quite literally, of an outpouring of energy between our parents. Our lives began with that fusion of two living cells, carrying a unique mix of genes, and energized by a power that we can perhaps, most truly, call 'desire'. The expression of that desire may have been less than ideal, human love being so painfully imperfect, but it remains a fact that the desire of one human being for another culminated in the conception of a third person. That is the story of every human being's beginning.

This is true whether or not the life which sprang from

that moment was intended or unplanned. And this too seems to tell us something about the nature of our 'energy cycles'. They begin with a life-giving moment, which is in some way an expression of desire. We could call it a 'sunspot'. And from then on they work themselves out in ways that could not have been predicted at the start, just as a child's life, once begun, will be lived out, quite regardless of whether the parents ever intended it or not.

Recognizing the 'sunspots'

Our own life cycles are worked out in a similar way. The energy released in the life-giving moment provides the power for the period of our lives that flows out of it and follows after. This becomes more obvious if you move on from that first beginning to later cycles in your life. Just to look back over the first twenty or thirty years of your life will begin to reveal a pattern. I experienced a strong 'life pulse', for example, around the age of seven or so, in my encounter with the transcendent splendour of the stars. For me it was a spiritual experience I have never forgotten, and the energy that flowed into me in that surge of joy and wonder has never left me.

For a friend of mine, now a scientist and a teacher, a crucial sunspot came when she was a small girl in school and was present to her first scientific experiment. As the various components surged into a new life when mixed together in the test tube, something new welled up inside her, and she knew that this was a sign pointing out her personal direction in life and giving her the overwhelming desire to follow that sign.

And sometimes our 'sunspots' seem to happen as a result of a decision we take for ourselves, reflecting a real point of commitment or intention. This might be, for example, the decision to marry or to commit to a partnership, or the decision to embark on a particular career, or take a new job, or to start a family.

Whatever the circumstances, such 'sunspots' seem to begin with the awakening of powerful desire, which then releases a surge of energy to fuel the onward journey. The phase of life which follows is then lived out and worked out in the power and in the light of the originating desire.

No doubt you can see similar patterns in your life so far, and if you are living in a partnership or in some form of community, you will probably notice the pattern of an energy burst in your decision to make a commitment to that partner or that community. Such commitment also, at its best, begins with desire, to be joined with that partner or community, and that desire is often expressed ritually in the ceremony of marriage or in a formal exchange of promises. The energy that is released from that desire then fuels the task of living out the consequences of those promises. A similar pattern can be seen in the desire to pursue a particular kind of work or the decision to have a child. We call decisions like these 'life-changing', because they are usually the starting point for a new phase of our lives, and we can say these things about them:

- They begin from desire;

- The desire results in a fresh outpouring of energy;

- The energy fuels the living out and working out of the initial desire;

- The surge of energy seems to be given for a purpose, which will be worked out in the years ahead.

A hilltop called Horeb

A story from the book of Exodus (chapter 3) describes a hilltop experience in the life of Moses. Moses was born to a Hebrew family at a time of persecution when all newborn Hebrew boys were under threat of death. So it was that he came to be hidden in a basket among the reeds in the river, where he was discovered by Pharaoh's daughter, and subsequently brought up in the Egyptian court. If Moses were making this journey with us now, he would probably identify his rescue by Pharaoh's daughter as his first 'sunspot' and an obvious 'life-giving moment' in his life.

And there were to be other major energy shifts ahead for him. One of them happened while he was looking after his father-in-law's flocks, near Horeb, which was considered to be a 'holy mountain'. We find him on this hilltop, which is sacred space for the whole community, both geographically and spiritually, and is about to become personal sacred space for Moses.

It was an ordinary day on the hillside, and Moses was looking after his father-in-law's very ordinary flocks. We might imagine him walking the hillside, noticing the dried-up grassy hillocks, examining the sparse growth of plants and bushes, and then scanning the distant skies, blue-white with the heat of the day, with just a few clusters of fleecy cloud relieving the monotony.

Then, just a few hundred yards away, a glimmer of fire. A crackle, as of burning twigs. Sometimes the shepherds would light small fires on the hillside, and brew themselves a pot of tea with the aromatic herbs that grew on Mount Horeb. But there was no sign of any other human presence here. Moses went closer to investigate.

The bush was on fire. There was no doubt about that. But it was not burning. It was not getting any less. On the contrary, it was becoming more and more vibrantly present, or so it seemed to Moses' wide-eyed gaze. And as he drew closer, he began to realize this was a special moment in his life. The whole ambience of the hillside seemed to be changing. Everything around him felt more real and looked more clear than it had done before. A moment of heightened awareness? Whatever was happening, he sensed that some barrier between the seen and the unseen had been breached, and he knew the energy that was setting the bush alight was creative, not destructive. It was bringing forth a significant change in his life, but as yet he had no idea of what that could be.

Moses was overawed. Within his terms of reference, such a feeling, such an experience, could only come from God. 'Come closer,' the bush seemed to invite him. He approached, in silent, expectant wonder, until the bush spoke again: 'Take off your sandals, for you are standing on holy ground.'

Then the source of the life-giving flame made itself known to Moses: 'I am the God of your ancestors, the God of Isaac and the God of Jacob.' And Moses covered his face, overwhelmed.

The sacred moment had been sealed, as God and Moses acknowledged its power and its meaning. Only then could God reveal its purpose. 'I have seen the misery in which my people are living,' he said. 'I have heard their cries of desperation in the face of so much oppression and heartache. I desire to free them from everything that enslaves them, and bring them to a place where their hearts can be eternally at home. Their cry for help has reached me. I am sending you to be their deliverer. And in everything you do I shall be with you. This burning bush is a sign of that promise. It burns with the energy of my constant presence and it is your spiritual fuel for the task that lies ahead of you. And when my people have been freed, they will come to this mountain, knowing it to be holy ground, because here God and humankind have met, a new vision has been opened up, and a new stage in my people's journey has begun.'

The meeting of God with Moses on Mount Horeb became a kind of transaction between them, entered into for the sake of the people in need of help. Our 'sunspots', too, can be like burning bushes. They have a lot in common with Moses' experience:

- They feel like moments when something very significant is breaking through into our lives;

- They feel creative, and not destructive, even though they may sometimes be very turbulent and even frightening;

- They often seem to draw us onward to a point of commitment, to a particular course of action or new direction in our lives;

- They are seen, with hindsight, to have had a wider purpose, which is not simply about our own well-being, but concerns the well-being of others.

We never forget our 'burning-bush' experiences. They become sacred space for us from then on. Every time we revisit them in memory, something of that initial burst of energy is experienced again, and keeps us going on with whatever it is we have undertaken.

Connecting to the mains

We may be able to detect, fairly clearly, the 'big-bang' sunspots that have provided a burst of energy to fuel a new phase of our lives. We may even be able to start to notice a 'seven-year' pattern that helps us to get in touch with the underlying currents of our heart's journey. These are our inner 'hilltops', giving us the vision and the energy to keep walking. We could call them our 'burning bushes'.

But the existence of electricity means nothing to us if we have no plugs and sockets. How do we earth this energy and take hold of its power in our lives?

The hilltops of our lives may indeed provide the vision of all we dream of and hope for, just as moments of falling in love, whether with another person, or with a vocation, or with life itself, open up the horizons of our hearts' dearest longings. But hills have to be climbed, and our visions have to become grounded and incarnate, if they are to become co-creative in God's Dream for creation. The love we feel must become the love we express and the love we turn into action. Thus 'falling in love' becomes, with the ripening of time, real covenant relationship, and 'inspiration' is shaped into a real project for a real world. This is what it means to 'realize' our potential. This process of realization can feel like the long hard climb along the mountainsides of our vision. It demands real effort, and it challenges us to travel light, and leave a good deal of our mental and emotional baggage behind us, in the valley, conserving our energy for making the dream reality.

Turning the ideals of our vision into the reality of everyday? Is it an idle dream? From the perspective of everyday human existence the 'ideal' and the 'real' seem to exist in different worlds. Sometimes it seems as though we are blessed with hundreds of 'ideals', but find no way, or no time, to turn even a few of them into reality. At other times we feel swamped by the 'real' and we wonder whatever happened to our ideals. Our hilltop vision seems to be lost in the fog of day-to-day survival.

The deadlock can be eased when we take hold of the fact

that our 'hilltops', the sites of our burning bushes, are the sources of our creative energy. Energy is not a static entity. By its very nature it *flows*, and on our spiritual journey it flows from our vision into our realization of that vision. We could say that it erupts on our 'hilltops', setting the bush of our dreaming alight, and then it flows right down into our valleys, bringing the hilltop energy into our lived experience.

So a few things might be worth pondering as we allow ourselves to reconnect to our dreaming:

● Where have I encountered my personal burning bushes, and what has each one of them meant to me? What vision was it heralding in my life?

● Using the energy released by that vision, how did I live out the dream in that stage of my life? How did that particular dream become incarnate? How do I feel about the results?

● Whether I now look back on that part of my journey as a 'success' or as a disappointment, it has certainly changed me in some way. I have grown through that experience, and moved a little closer to becoming who I really am. How do I feel about that growth and change?

Take a little time (perhaps alone in your 'inner space') to reflect on the burning bushes you have encountered on your own hilltops so far. Look into their flames. What particular dream or vision or hope do those flames reveal? When you encountered them, what were you most deeply desiring? Perhaps it was to gain an important qualification, to make an important journey, to make a life commitment to someone you loved, to make a home, to raise a child, to bring a special project to fulfilment? Notice those specific dreams you have had. Let yourself connect to the energy they generated in your life. Can you see how that energy turned into tangible results? If you gained that qualification, for example, how did that shape the years which followed?

If any of your dreams has appeared to end in disappointment, don't throw it away! Receive it now into your sacred space, and let it show you how the experience of that disappointment has also shaped the years which followed. Probably, if you can distance yourself from the immediate pain of it, you can begin to notice how that difficult time has helped to form you into who you really are, more surely than the easier conquests might have done. In whichever direction the flames of a particular burning bush have directed you, the years which followed have been a crucial stage of your personal 'Becoming'. They are part of the realization of your inner dream.

One of the great gifts of our hilltops is that of *perspective*. The world looks different from the top of a hill. The sweat and struggle of each little field of effort is seen to be part of a much larger landscape. The failed crop of one year becomes the nourishment for the growth of the next season. Go back, as often as you feel the need, to that inner hilltop and let it connect you to the larger patterns of your living. Then let it recharge you with the inner resources to descend again into the valley and to keep going along your way.

Coming down the mountain

Many people who walk the hills and climb the mountains of our world can be heard to complain that the coming down is harder work than the going up. Personally, I know that the climbing up challenges my lungs, while the climbing down takes its toll on my knees. Moreover, the climbing up is usually done in the prime of the day when our energy is at its height, and when we are inspired and motivated by the hope of the view from the summit cairn. The journey down usually happens when we are tired, and when we may feel we have had to leave something behind us at the summit that we would like to have stayed with for ever.

We are not the first to feel this way. You might like to come back through time for a while and join another little band of hikers in first-century Palestine, as they take a morning walk up a mountain called Tabor, as described in Matthew's Gospel, chapter 17. There are four of them – Jesus of Nazareth and three of his friends, Peter, James and John. This is a retelling of how the walk goes:

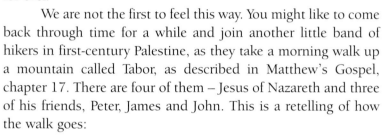

Jesus took Peter, James and John, his friends, and led them with him to the mountain called Tabor. The four of them were alone, as they made their way that morning to the summit. Perhaps they too were looking forward to the view from the top. Perhaps they savoured the crisp dawn air as they climbed, maybe in silence, maybe in friendly conversation.

The view from the top was indeed going to be breathtaking. Far from gazing down over the panorama below them, their gaze was drawn to Jesus himself. Even as they gazed, he seemed to become suffused with light and a deep radiance, penetrating them with its own warmth. Even his clothing shone, as if some eternal fire were burning within him, making his whole being come alive in ways beyond imagination. They had sometimes seen a person's face light up in this way in the presence of some great joy, but this man's whole being was on fire. What kind of joy could kindle a fire like that, they wondered?

Then the scene widened, and they became aware of two other figures standing beside Jesus in this pool of light. Two of their people's most revered ancestors and prophet–leaders, Moses and Elijah, were there, talking with him. It was as though this moment was being lived out of time and space, in the place where all is One. They were standing in time, yet seeing eternity; standing in a finite place, yet touching the infinite, where all the walls and compartments of human thinking had dissolved.

Peter was the first to speak. 'Lord,' he said, 'this is such an amazing moment of vision. I will build three shrines here, one for you, one for Moses and one for Elijah, so that we can hold on to this vision for ever.' But he never finished his sentence, because a cloud came down over the scene, and out of the cloud the watching friends seemed to hear words being spoken: 'This is my Son; this is One who is at home and unchanging, with me in the All-One, yet present with you in the finite, changing spaces of creation.' And then a word of warning: 'Don't try to contain this vision in your man-made shrines, but listen to the truth it speaks to your heart.' Then the cloud faded, and the hilltop was as it had always been. They felt, once more, the warm touch of Jesus' hand upon them and heard him say, 'Don't be afraid.' And he led them back down the mountain, to carry all they had witnessed back to life in the valley.

Perhaps our own 'hilltop' experiences are less dramatic than this, yet surely they are characterized by the same qualities:

- They expose us to a burst of creative energy capable of fuelling the next stage of our onward journey;

- They take us momentarily beyond time and space and open up to us the horizons of eternity, calling us to translate these horizons into real vision in a real world;

- They cannot be held on to. They demand of us that we move on, that we walk back down to the valleys of our daily lives, there to live in the power and live out the vision of what we have seen and known at the summit.

From springtime to fall

The descent from our mountaintop moments reminds us that every cycle of our lives comes to an end. This is where the initial desire which set the cycle in motion has to turn into detachment, and the necessity to 'let go'. Just as every cycle of our lives has its unique and particular springtime, bringing that initial burst of energy, so too each cycle has its autumn, its fall, its time of coming down from the heights.

This cycle reflects the nature of the trees, and *where they direct their energy*. In spring all their life-force seems to flow into the rising sap, the buds and the fresh leaves, the supple young branches, the new growth. And then in winter the direction of that energy seems to turn, down to the roots, so that the tree might survive, and deepen its hold on life.

And I notice in my own life that the flow, or direction, of my energy seems to change according to which 'season' of my life I have reached and whether I am at the beginning or the end of one of my energy cycles. You may find it helpful, as I do, to look at your 'energy map' as if you were looking at a tree.

It is easy to notice the above-ground part. What do your branches look like? Where is your life energy mainly flowing? Perhaps to your family, your work, your career, a particular interest or passionate concern – peace and justice, the environment, helping a charity or making a home. In their own way these things are all about *growth*, and *reaching out*. In the tree's terms, they are 'springtime things'.

Now choose one of those branches – the strongest maybe. What leaves does it have? How does your involvement in that particular 'branch' express itself in real life? A completed project, perhaps. A child raised. A house built. An exam passed. A qualification gained. Funds raised for a charity. You could see all these things as your achievements, or at least as the things you want to achieve.

Relationships are another way in which the tree reveals itself in leaves. Some may be beautiful, some may be blighted. But the fact of autumn is that all of them will fall. *How do you feel* about that falling? Children will grow up and leave home. Friends will die. Projects will flourish, or fail, but will eventually slip into memory, and into forgetfulness. The universe will outlive all our achievements, and even the universe is not immortal. *How do you feel about this?*

The tree can help us to understand the need to come down from our various hilltop experiences, in order to let their power take deeper root. How might a tree feel when autumn comes, if it could express its feelings? It has to surrender its beauty when it is at its most radiant. Our children, too, usually leave home just at the prime of their lives. Letting them go can be one of the hardest things we have to do, yet we all know that such letting go is essential to the continuance of life.

So, into this blaze of glory, the cold winds and the November rains come. Those very things that we thought were 'our crowning glory' disappear into the autumn mists. Our radiance sinks down into leaf mould. When we think of having to let these things go, most of us realize, too well, how much we long to cling to them.

What does the tree do? If it possessed consciousness, it would surely recognize its helplessness to change this cycle of flowering and falling. In fact, what the tree does is a simple, vivid model of the art of letting go. It lets the leaves fall, and directs its energy *downwards* – to its roots, to the soil that provides its nutrients and its support. The tree turns its focus to the earth, which is, quite literally, *the ground of its being.*

As for all created things, the energy of the tree is limited and finite. Given just the meagre winter supply of energy (from the diminished warmth and daylight), where does it make sense to direct that energy? Out to the leaves or down to the root?

Now, in the light of this pattern of hilltops and valleys, of rising and falling, of springtime and fall, ask yourself: Where is the 'real you' most deeply centred? In your 'leaves', your 'branches', your 'trunk' or your 'roots', which are the deep centre of yourself and the source of everything you are? If you only have the energy to keep one part of your being alive, which part will you choose – one of the leaves, one of the branches, or the tap root? We might think about what would happen if the tree in winter could decide, instead, to 'stay with the leaves'. Eventually the roots would become so deprived of energy that they would shrivel. The tree would die. And the leaves it so longed to hold on to would fall anyway.

Letting go is the process of descending from our hilltops. In terms of the tree, it is not about despising or rejecting our God-given 'leaves'. But it *is* about recognizing what is most in tune with each part of our life cycles. It is about recognizing what, at any particular stage in our 'Becoming', is *essential* to our inner lives, and being prepared, if necessary, to let everything else be subordinated to the overriding choice for what is growing us into who we really are. It is a call to recognize the 'ground of our being', just as the tree does.

This choosing works itself out in hundreds of choices, large and small, that we make day by day. The call to let go is really a call to reflect, in every such moment of choosing and deciding: Which choice, which course of action, is *more* likely to lead to a deepening of my truest self and a closer bonding with the truest self of every other creature and of all creation?

Of course, we will often fail to 'choose the roots', but every time we choose well, our discernment will grow a little bit sharper and our lives become a little bit more focused than they were before. Gradually the whole tree of our own life and of the life of all creation will be strengthened and enriched, and next year's leaves and next year's fruit will be all the more radiant and nutritious. Far from losing the leaves we have surrendered, we will find we have gained a wholeness and a deep-down health of spirit, and a freedom that opens the channels of our hearts to the 'sap' of Life itself, holding us in being.

When we can reach this kind of balance, then we are ready to face the winter, and the bare branches and the cold winds. I remember one year when I was making my first retreat. On my window sill was a vase of sweet peas. In the beginning they were a source of great joy to me, filling my room with their fragrance. Then, as the days of retreat passed, gradually the petals began to fall, until, on the last day, they all lay lifeless on the sill. It reminded me that this special time in retreat was coming to an end. Then I noticed the silky pod that still remained on the stalk. With a shaft of renewed joy I recognized the flower's seedpod. The seeds of tomorrow were revealed only when the petals of today had been let go.

And, as I reflect on this memory, I realize that in some mysterious way, the apparent ending of every creative cycle in my own life has also been the gateway to the next inpouring of creative energy. Organized religion, in most of its forms, has formalized this intuition into stories of death and resurrection, all of which are saying, in their own way, 'Descend from the hilltop, when the time is right, and trust the valley's dying, because this is the beginning of new life.'

Listening to the heartbeat of God

One simple way of turning towards the ground of your being, and coming into resonance with your deepest self, is to place your finger upon your own pulse. You might like to try this. Feel the regular, rhythmic throb. Every throb is a 'life-giving moment' for your physical being. If those throbs fail, you die. Then let those pulse beats draw you back to the more spaced-out throbs of life-giving energy that you have become aware of in the cycles and phases of your particular, personal life. Go back to your own beginnings, and to that impulse of desire which brought you into being in your mother's womb.

Then further back still, right back to that initial burst of cosmic energy that first thrust our universe into being. And perhaps our universe is one among many, and there was an even Bigger Bang before all that, far beyond all our perceptions.

When I let myself travel back through time and space in this way, I feel somehow connected to the very heartbeat of God. Every deep, inner 'life moment' that I recognize, perhaps in prayer, or dream, or an unexpected encounter with another creature, releases a little surge of inner energy that defines and sustains the time which follows it. And I feel sure that when God touches any one of us with such a moment, he touches all of us.

When I stand with my finger on my pulse, and my heart turned to God (whatever name I give 'him'), it feels as if the whole of our universe, bearing all the secret seeds of every being that shall come to be, is like a single heartbeat of God. I have an overwhelming sense, not only of the immeasurable difference in time between God's single massive heartbeats of creative energy, and my own second-by-second life pulses, but also of the absolute connectedness, the intimate relatedness between them. One heartbeat of God can set a universe in motion. One heartbeat of mine can keep me in being for just a single moment. Yet, deep down, the two are one, and my pulse is just a distant echo of his, carrying his life energy to the minutest cells and fibres of my personal being.

What we call prayer is, perhaps, nothing more (and nothing less!) than to be in the resonance that exists eternally between the heartbeat of the creator and the pulse throbs and life-giving moments in his creature. The difference is only one of timescale. My pulse, and yours, is God's pulse, speeded up. His pulse is yours and mine, immeasurably amplified. To speak of God's heartbeat may sound like mere sentiment, yet here it is, beating in our own bodies, not just metaphor and emotion, but a real, solid heartbeat that quite literally pumps life and energy, visible and invisible, through creation. When this living Spirit beats in us, we live. If that pulse is withheld, we die.

If we look with open eyes we can see the outworkings of that pulsing in the energy cycles of our lives. We can observe something of the big 'seven-year cycles' in our lives, with their own 'big bangs', right down to the tiniest of 'big bangs' that happens every time our own hearts beat, resonating in every throb of our pulses, pumping life energy through our bodies. And the same pattern appears in those spiritual life moments that set off each new creative phase in us. They are echoed, and can be nourished, in more regular inner energy surges that flow, for example, from times of retreat, or days of recollection, or hours of deliberate stillness – right down to the minute-by-minute life moments of simply becoming aware of this invisible life and presence in all parts of creation.

This, it seems to me, is true *heart* knowledge, and when life and circumstances drive me into a state of hypertension, I can do something about it. I can stop, and in the stillness I can listen to my own racing pulse. I can tune in to the distant echo of the one eternal heartbeat that steadies my frenzy, into God's stillness.

Seasons of setting out

At this station on our Way, we remember and celebrate the commitments we have made to our particular life choices and relationships. These have been times of setting out upon new visions, fired by the desire to grow and bear fruit in specific ways.

On days of special significance or celebration, it is not uncommon for bonfires to be lit on hilltops, and for bells to peal out across the countryside. These gestures create a kind of chain reaction. To be present to them makes us feel part of a great continuum which began beyond our horizons, and extends forward beyond what we can imagine. Thus a local bonfire or the bells of the parish church become part of something larger, encircling a whole region and connecting people together in a powerful bond, like an Olympic flame, passing from hand to hand.

You might like to take a look back over your personal hilltops in this kind of way. On each of them you have made some kind of commitment. Perhaps you celebrated this landmark at the time, maybe with a family party or a solemn ritual of undertaking. Just call to mind now those hilltops that have defined your life's landscape so far.

- What did they mean to you?

- How did you mark them?

- What was your vision as you embarked on each new phase of your life?

- How has it been worked out in practice?

- How has it affected those around you, and the rest of creation?

Sealing your promises

Many of our life commitments are sealed in some formal way, perhaps in an exchange of promises, or in the signing of a contract. This fact in itself indicates something of the importance we attach to our commitments, as a human community.

You may well find, however, that some of the hilltops you have discovered at this station have not been the conventional life commitments you expected. Yet they too are worthy of celebration. They too ask to be sealed.

One way to do this is to ask yourself where you feel you are in your life right now. Is there a hilltop in sight? You may be standing on one even now, or you may just have passed one or feel you are just approaching another. Reflect on what that hilltop is about:

- What is the view from its summit?

- What kind of energy does it seem to be generating in you?

- Where do you hope that energy will lead?

- Which other people are most closely involved in your vision for this stage of your life?

- How do you hope your vision will affect them?

Now that you have become fully aware of your hilltop vision, you might like to 'seal' it in one or more of these ways:

- By sharing it with a friend, to whom you can tell your hopes and dreams – and your fears;

- By choosing some symbol or marker that will remind you, every day, of that vision and how you hope to live it out;

- By recording your feelings and the nature of your commitment to this particular vision, either in a notebook, or in a letter to yourself (fascinating reading for later years!), or in a diary or scrapbook, or even on tape or video;

- By noticing, as time goes on, just how the initial energy of your commitment has been worked out in practice, and what fruits it has borne, for yourself and for others.

Commitments such as marriage, or the start of a new job, are usually marked in these ways: by sharing them publicly in some way; by incorporating some symbol of the commitment (a ring, for example) into daily life; and by formalizing the covenant agreement in writing. There is no reason why other kinds of serious undertaking, and the embracing of a new phase of life, should not be similarly honoured.

Some of our commitments survive, others fail. Don't just abandon your disappointments. Whether you feel you have 'failed' or 'succeeded' in any particular venture, the time will come for the letting go. When you reach this stage of a cycle, it can be healing and ultimately life-giving to commit it back to the earth, to the ground of your being, just as the tree lets the leaves fall. Don't be afraid to 'bury' your hopes and dreams, when they have lived out their life, for better or for worse. But when you do (and in whatever ritualized way) take with you a seed of your next dream, your next hilltop hope, and plant it on the burial site. For in every ending is the new beginning, and the two cannot be separated.

wells

POOLS OF POSSIBILITY

When I was a child my parents' house backed onto a wood. Every April this wood was carpeted with bluebells. As young as seven years old I felt I knew every square foot of it. Through an isolated childhood, with neither siblings nor close neighbours, the bluebell wood was my playground. I had a place of my own in the depths of the woods, a grassy hollow that became my den. I furnished it with bits of stick, with brambles and rose-hips, and an occasional jam jar of bluebells when they were in season, and I was sure that God lived in my wood, and was especially present in my little hollow. I used to write him notes, asking for his company on the dangerous missions that haunted my extreme youth, such as those daunting birthday parties, or a summons to the head teacher. And sometimes I just wrote to say, 'Hello,' and let him know how I was feeling.

The hollow became sacred space for me, and as the months and years passed I felt more and more at home there. Perhaps I even sanctified it, by believing in its benevolence.

It was many years later, long after I had reached the age of reason and abandoned my childhood intimacy with the God of the woods, that I found out my sacred hollow was actually an old bomb crater. When I had first discovered it, this grass-covered oasis was hazardously fresh, a mere half-dozen years after the cessation of the Second World War and the bombing raids over my home town. My sacred space, that only God and I knew about, may well have been concealing an unexploded bomb.

Bombs among the bluebells

When I return, in memory, to this wooded hollow, I often reflect on the strange relationship there seems to be between what is most creative in our lives and what is, potentially, most destructive. It reminds me that to live life in all its fullness is to journey constantly in the company of risk that will challenge me beyond my 'comfort zone'. I know that I can fall into the depths, as readily, if not more so, as I rise to the heights of my experience. I have come to recognize that joy and sorrow are two sides of a single coin, and my angels and demons walk hand in hand.

A well, which the Celts revered as sacred space, expresses something of this paradox. It is sacred because it is the source of water, the cradle and assurance of life itself. Yet that source of life is only reached by descending into the depths of a deep, dark shaft.

At this fourth station on our Celtic Way we pause to reflect on these depths. Not all of our memories are charged with the energy of joy. Some carry energy that feels destructive and negative. Yet these 'wells' of our lives may be the very place from which we draw living water.

At this station we are, significantly, at the mid-point of our pilgrimage. We might define this mid-point as that moment when the bucket of our lives touches the bottom of the well of our experience, just before it turns once more, to ascend towards the light. To risk the journey to the bottom of the well demands courage. For many of us, that journey into darkness only happens when circumstances force us into an encounter with 'rock bottom'. Must such an encounter be negative? Or might the dark shaft of the well truly bring us to 'sacred space'?

Today, especially in urban areas, the notion of a well may be something we have only gleaned from fairy tales or distant rural idylls. Yet if a well is a shaft of darkness through which we must travel in order to discover new means of life, then our city deserts and urban wastelands would seem to be full of such places of encounter. Perhaps I might share with you a recent experience at the bottom of a city 'well', in a subway garden dug deep below an arterial road. It may have the power to remind you of your own 'wells', and the buds of new life that may be sprouting in their depths.

A city well

The day took off in a hurry. I began it by oversleeping, and then had to rush to town to do some business at the bank. Otherwise it was an altogether unremarkable morning in late April. I parked at the supermarket and made my way to the bank by the quickest route, crossing the still-empty market place. Then something stopped me. Every morning that spring I had driven round the roundabout in the centre of town, noticing the blossom bursting into life on the trees planted down there in the subway oasis at its centre, and being quietly grateful for the spring flowers girding the island. I had kept telling myself I must find a moment to go down there and enjoy the flowers and the blossom more wholeheartedly. I suddenly had the urge to do just that – to take the longer route back to the car park, via the subway gardens.

All the haste of the day left me, for a few blessed moments. Instead of taking the short arc of the path encircling the sunken garden, I deliberately chose the longer arc, but

halfway round it, I couldn't go on. I knew that I had to spend some real time there, not merely a quick dip snatched from the jaws of a busy day. I settled myself on one of the benches, just for long enough to become more deeply aware of everything that was around me – not only the lovely flowers and the blossoming trees, but the people passing through, and the buses and juggernauts circling above me, round the roundabout.

As the artificial urgency of the morning gradually drained away, I began to realize that there was something steady and still in the middle of all the running round in circles, the noise and clamour, the dangers and the distractions. I was sitting at a still point, surrounded by the whirlpool of life. I could feel my heart relaxing.

It occurred to me that I was the only person sitting there, on one of the many benches. Other people were constantly passing through, but almost no one stopped. Later the subway garden would become populated by the little community of drunks and 'down-and-outs' who would settle here on these benches as the day progressed. Strange, I reflected, that we sometimes have to be 'down' and 'out', and 'running on empty' before we stop to fill up from the pure wells, like this, in the middle of our cities. How often we have to find ourselves with nothing left to lose, before we discover we have everything to gain.

An elderly man, with a huge, dishevelled beard, wandered in, carrying a plastic carrier bag. He stopped close by and picked up some old bread crusts that were lying discarded among the flowers. For an instant I thought he was collecting them for himself, gathering a thrown-away meal in his carrier bag. But no – he laid the bag to one side, and broke up all the crusts into little, bite-sized pieces, then threw them into the bushes, for the birds. I watched as he celebrated a genuine act of communion with the hungry sparrows. He was breaking bread with them, and I knew I was witnessing a sacramental moment. He had time that morning. And he had time for the rest of creation. He was part of the pure water that the well was yielding. And, undoubtedly, he was an eccentric. Only the eccentrics, or the desperate, would fall out of the circle of juggernauts, travelling the endless roundabout of life above us.

Five minutes later a young man came through, walking fast and purposefully, carrying a boxed microwave oven on his shoulder. The fast-food man only just missed the slow feeder-of-birds. I wondered how much else he only just misses.

A young couple passed by, hand in hand, but looking as if they were walking together into a great sorrow, their expressions heavy with some unspoken apprehension. I could almost feel their pain, as they passed by, slowly and thoughtfully. It seemed to me, down there, that the slower you went, the more deeply the place could touch you.

And then the realization began to dawn that this was the bottom of a well. This was where people might come who have reached the end of their resources. A place people drop into when they fall out of life's circle of busyness. Perhaps they only come for a respite moment in a busy day's shopping. Or perhaps they drop into this well through a trapdoor of despair. But when they do, and for whatever reason, they might find themselves at the gate of heaven, if only for one brief moment of awareness. Because down there, in the well, on such an April morning, every flower shouts for life, and the birdsong resonates more purely and persistently than the pounding of the juggernauts. Can the well of our despair really become a source of living water?

Perhaps the Celts revered wells as 'sacred space' because they enable us to draw life-giving water from the depths of the earth. Our experience goes 'down' as well as 'up'. Down to the depths of pain and darkness as well as up to the hilltop summits of energy and vision.

As you take time now to look deep into some of the shafts of your life, you might like to bring to mind any times when you have felt 'at the bottom of the well'. Without any kind of judgment, of yourself or of others, just acknowledge your memories and let them be there. And, trusting that the Celtic intuition is true, and that you are indeed standing in sacred space, risk letting the bucket go down into the dark shaft, in search of that living water. Risk the dive, in the possibility that there may be treasure in the shipwreck.

Cul-de-sacs and turning places

Logically, every well ought to have a 'No Through Road' sign at its head. One thing is sure, that at the bottom of the well there is no other way than 'up'. A well, then, is not just a source of water, but also a place of *turning*.

Sometimes the plunge into the well can be dramatic and terrifying. This is how it was for a rather spoiled seventeen-year-old boy called Joseph, who found himself very suddenly, and painfully, over the edges of his 'comfort zone' one day. The story is told in the book of Genesis, chapters 37 to 45.

Joseph was a child of what we might call a dysfunctional family, fraught by multiple marriages and the resulting rivalries between stepchildren. We find him out in the fields, looking after his father Jacob's flocks, and carrying home unsavoury tales about the conduct of his stepbrothers. Jacob makes no secret of his favouritism of Joseph. He has just given him a present – a special coat, beautifully decorated. But Joseph's enjoyment of his gift is to be short-lived.

The coat becomes the spark that sets alight the tinder of his half-brothers' seething resentment of him, and fuels their jealousy to fever pitch. They have reached the end of their tolerance of his arrogant behaviour towards them. The situation is an explosion waiting to happen. On the fateful morning, Jacob sends Joseph off to Shechem, where the flocks are pastured, to check on how the brothers are doing. They see him coming before he sees them. They are ready for him, with a plan to get rid of this thorn in their flesh for ever.

'Let's kill him,' they murmur, 'and throw his body down the well. We'll say he was eaten by a wild animal.' It is Reuben who persuades his brothers against this act of murder, and gets them to commute Joseph's sentence, and throw him into the well alive, meaning to rescue him later. Unfortunately, as for so many good intentions, 'later' never comes, because before Reuben can save Joseph, a band of merchants passes by and Joseph is sold into

slavery in Egypt. So it happens that Joseph finds himself in the household of one of the chief henchmen of Pharaoh, the ruler of the Egyptian oppressors.

Over the years that follow, Joseph's fortunes fluctuate wildly. Sometimes he enjoys the favour of the court, and sometimes not, but eventually he gains something of a reputation as an interpreter of dreams, and also as a shrewd business manager. Pharaoh is so impressed by what he sees that he appoints Joseph as the governor of all Egypt, with the power, among other things, to manage the distribution of the food supplies. So, with the foresight of the dreamer and the businessman combined, Joseph arranges to save an abundance of corn in the years of plenty, in the light of his intuition that a time of famine is looming.

The time comes, inevitably, when his own half-brothers are sent to Egypt, desperately looking for food. They are brought before Joseph, who now has his would-be executioners in his power, but of course they no longer recognize him. As might be expected, Joseph does not miss out on this opportunity for a few games of cat and mouse with them, before revealing his true identity and giving them, freely, the food they have come to buy.

Perhaps, however, the real heart of this story, and the moment which shows how the bucket has reached the bottom of the well and turned round again, is captured in Joseph's words to his alienated family:

'Come closer to me. I am your brother, the one you sold into slavery. But don't grieve over that now. Don't reproach yourselves for what is in the past. Now we can see that God used these terrible circumstances to send me ahead of you, here into Egypt, into enemy territory, to open up a channel of possibility that would eventually save your lives. And this is about more than just our own family. My presence here, by the chance of bad circumstance, has been turned into a way of keeping all of our race alive through this famine. Because of what happened all those years ago at the well, I have access to all the food supplies of the region and no one shall die of hunger while I live.'

This is a quite amazing turnaround. Not only have the fortunes of Jacob's family, and the people of Israel, been transformed, and their lives saved, but perhaps even more significantly, Joseph's youthful arrogance has been turned into genuine compassion, and a humble recognition that God has brought great good out of something so potentially destructive. The bucket of family tension and jealous hatred has gone right down to the bottom of that empty well, into which they pitched their brother, and has surfaced once again, bringing the means of new life for everyone in the region.

So the well of despair and destructiveness can become something life-giving, and in ways we cannot possibly predict – or even believe in – when we feel our lives have reached rock bottom. The bottom of the well can become a place of turning, and a place of conversion, and it is this potential for miracle that can make it into sacred space. The place of our most abject poverty can become a place of resurrection.

The place of poverty and the place of resurrection

Pilgrimage has a destination, and Celtic pilgrimage historically names its destination as 'the place of resurrection'. For the Celtic wayfarer, the 'place of resurrection' was sensed to be a space of deep awareness of the harmony and wholeness of all things, as well as, quite literally, a place in which to settle, physically and spiritually, to await the fullness of life and experience, and to prepare for death as the gateway to new life, the end of the old cycle and the beginning of a new.

Paradoxically, this place of resurrection was frequently a place of hardship. The Celtic pilgrim would not be afraid to embrace the suffering, as one might embrace the pain of childbirth in the certain trust that it is the bringer of new life. While we might be less convinced of the virtue of hardship for its own sake, we can nevertheless share with our Celtic forebears the experience that sometimes the rock bottom of life opens up into a new phase of growth and maturing. When we reflect on our own stories, we find those turning points which, like Joseph's, have reversed our downward spiralling and brought new insight or new strength, not just for ourselves, but for others.

At our first station we pondered the interweaving of the infinite knot. Here, at the bottom of the well, and the place of turning, we find another reflection of that interwovenness. We find our worst entwined with our best, our despair with our hope, our shame with our glory. How might we engage, in practice, with this dark place of paradox? We might find a clue just a few miles from where I live, in the Derbyshire village of Eyam.

In this area, the Pennine hills of northern England, there is a time-honoured tradition of well-dressing. This goes back to the seventeenth century when the population of the region was decimated by the bubonic plague. Today, over 300 years later, the villagers still decorate their wells each year with intricate tableaux of flowers depicting biblical scenes, to express their gratitude for being alive, when surrounded by so much death.

The village of Eyam was caught in the sweep of the killer epidemic in 1665. In a communal act of selflessness the villagers agreed to isolate themselves, in an effort to protect the neighbouring settlements from contagion. They marked out their isolation perimeter by a circle of boundary stones, one of which was also a well. People from the surrounding area brought food, medication and news to these boundary markers and left them there to be collected by the stricken villagers.

It doesn't take too great a leap of the imagination to picture the remaining uninfected members of a family trudging to the boundary well, seeking the means of living for another day. This well must have become a powerful symbol of everything that wells are supposed to be – everything that makes them 'sacred space' – a symbol of the source of life, of healing and of cleansing from contagion.

Now, so many centuries later, the flower-bedecked wells of Derbyshire continue to proclaim that the place of death and devastation is also the place of a resurrection of the human spirit of courage and selflessness, and a determination that life, not death, shall prevail. Hundreds of thousands of tourists – or

should we more rightly call them pilgrims – flock to these villages every year. The space these wells represent has become sacred, by common consent. The Celts would have recognized this intuition.

And so, in Eyam, we find a story of how the human spirit can discover its place of resurrection by entering the heart of the darkness, without evasion or circumvention.

Neglected wells

Today, in the age of mains-water supplies, when our spring water comes to us in plastic bottles, many wells are neglected and overgrown. Very few are still used for their original purpose. Those that are tend to become museum pieces and 'attractions' on a tourist leaflet.

Much more seriously, perhaps, the deepest wells and the darkest shafts of human experience are likewise all too easily overgrown and set aside as undesirable and unnecessary. Almost everything in our Western culture transmits the continual message that to live fully is to be comfortable, satisfied and free from pain. We treat the symptoms of our deeper hurting with the analgesics of pleasure and politeness, and we carefully avoid the thoughts and conversations that might tip us into the well.

Did the Celts, then – and so many other wayfarers before us – get it wrong? Are the dark places of our experience better ignored and discounted, or are they, on the contrary, a sacred space in which we will discover who we truly are?

There are many levels of response to the darkness within us:

- We can choose to board up our 'wells', as dangerous places from which we must protect ourselves. We can live at this level by studiously avoiding any conscious thought about the darker places of our souls and maintaining conversations that never go below the surface of our experience. If we do this, we also, very effectively, block the way for others to explore their deeper reaches with us.

- We can choose to dress our wells with flowers from time to time and revere them only for the memories they contain of times when we have come through the darkness. This is a bolder response, but it still focuses on our ability to overcome the darkness, rather than the ultimately life-giving truths about ourselves that the darkness would reveal if we dared to enter it fully.

- Or we can choose to risk the dark drop into the places we most fear within our hearts and lives, to discover for ourselves whether there is living water at the bottom of the shaft. This will rarely be a choice made willingly in the full light of day, but it can be an open-hearted response to the times when life plunges us to the depths through circumstances we are unable to avoid. It is said that the place we most fear is the place where we discover the true measure of our courage. The relationships which cause us the greatest heartache may be the wells from which we are drawing genuine growth in love and understanding.

In her book, *Away*, Jane Urquhart enters into the lives of Irish immigrants struggling in nineteenth-century Canada to wrest a living from the unyielding landscape of the Canadian Shield. For years they live in the extreme poverty of subsistence farming that barely keeps them alive. 'How's a man supposed to farm,' one of them asks, 'when under everything there's all this rock?' We might ask the same question sometimes of our own lives' landscape. Our poverty may not be material, but emotional or spiritual. Our empty barren places may be in the aching depths of our longings and our deepest disappointments. How are we supposed to live full lives, we might ask ourselves, with all this hard rock of pain underneath?

In *Away*, the answer comes, tragically, too late to prevent the hapless immigrants from abandoning this apparently fruitless place, and 'boarding up their well'. Too late, the hard rock yields up its secret: iron ore, marble – and gold!

Take a moment to reflect on the place where you feel your life is most empty and unyielding. Let yourself see how you are trying to farm this place, and make it bearable, but how often you feel this effort is futile. Notice, without judgment, your own desires to abandon the effort and look for easier living elsewhere. Finally, simply rest in the *possibility* that your place of poverty might hold gold hidden in its depths.

If this exercise seems impossible for you where you find yourself right now, try it retrospectively. Can you remember a 'place of poverty' in the past? Perhaps a set of circumstances that seemed hostile to you, or a big disappointment that may have derailed your plans and hopes and forced you down a different road? Now, with the wisdom of hindsight, can you see any seams of gold embedded in that hard rock?

In Jane Urquhart's book, the people of the Canadian Shield call the gold 'particles of broken lightning'. Have the storms of your own life exposed you to any flashes of lightning that seemed terrifyingly destructive at the time, but, over time, have turned into seams of gold in the depths of your soul?

A bitter chalice or a cup of life?

And so we stand at the pivot point of our pilgrimage. When we look into the darkness of the well's deep shaft, we feel afraid. If it were not so, we would be less than human.

A cherished fellow traveller of mine has often warned me that '*fear* and imagination are a lethal cocktail'. When we gaze into the place of fear, we can so easily imagine worse and worse outcomes of what we fear. However, when, in any given situation, we reach the bottom of the well, there is nothing left to fear, because (at least in this particular issue) we have faced the worst within ourselves, and the deadly downward spiral is halted. We can turn this warning round and see how it becomes a promise.

If fear and imagination, together, wreak such havoc, what might *love* and imagination, together, bring to birth? The highest ideals of our dreaming become possibilities, when love and imagination come together. The bucket is coming back up the well, and bringing fresh and living water.

Yet this point of turning depends always on our own choosing. The choice seems to lie in our own attitude to the dark depths of the well. We can see the darkness and the emptiness as a tomb-like space, with the capacity to devour and destroy us. Or we can choose to see the dark emptiness as that of a womb, with the potential to give birth to something new.

We can sometimes change tomb to womb by our own attitudes – by our choice to focus on any gleams of love and hope we find in the situation, rather than on the cold heaviness of our fears. Such a change in the direction of our focus can turn the lethal cocktail into a fountain of life. Sometimes the encounter with the bottom of the well can be an opportunity for reappraisal, and perhaps for choosing a different route forward from the one we had planned.

And sometimes, what for ourselves may taste like a bitter chalice may be a cup of life for others. Most of us will know, for example, someone who has a special kind of empathy for others who are in some kind of distress, and if we look more deeply we will usually find that such empathy has grown out of that person's own experience of darkness and sorrow. The only people who can truly empathize with, say, addiction, or serious illness, or bereavement, are the ones who have walked these paths themselves, and have come through the darkness and created space in their hearts for others to enter and find loving acceptance.

Human history shows us, over and over again, that in the worst eruptions of conflict and brutality, there are always fragile, but resilient threads of quiet courage and unsung heroism running through every situation like seams of gold from broken lightning. We can choose, day after day, whether to focus on the storms or on the gold.

Claiming the living water

The draught of living water can take us by surprise, and may be offered to us in the most unexpected places.

We met Jacob's favourite son earlier in this chapter, and learned with him something of the hard reality of life at the bottom of a well. Jacob's well appears again, centuries later, in John's Gospel (chapter 4), to finish its story:

It is a hot, dusty day in high summer. The land is parched and dry. A group of friends is walking through the countryside of a foreign region. They are tired, and hungry, and very, very thirsty. They stop beside a well. It is an ancient well that has stood there for many generations. The people from the next village have to come out here every morning and every night to fetch the water they need for living.

One of the group, the leader, sits down on the edge of the well. The others set off to the village to buy some food for their lunch. For a few minutes the leader of the group is alone there, watching his friends disappearing into the midday haze, off to the village. He wipes the sweat from his forehead and looks up. A woman is approaching, with a water jar, to draw water from the well. It is not the thing to do, to talk to a strange woman, especially in this foreign, hostile region. He knows that, but still he does not hesitate to draw her into conversation.

'Please will you give me a drink of water?' he asks her.

Her face registers shocked surprise that he should address her in this way, and she blurts out her response:

'You're foreign here, and our countries are implacable enemies. Your people wouldn't normally even use the same cups and bowls that one of my people had used.'

'If only you were able to see the truth of things below the visible surface,' he says to her. 'If you could, you would know yourself, and you would know and recognize the real me, and you wouldn't be shocked or afraid. You would find a well of life itself in my heart, and in your own.'

'I don't understand,' she replies. 'You have come to my ancestors' well here, without even a bucket. Where is this well of life supposed to be? This well was given to us by Jacob, our ancestor. He and his sons and his flocks all drank from it. Are you saying you know some secret about it that he didn't?'

The stranger is silent for a moment or two, before replying, 'When we drink the water from this well, we know that we will become thirsty again before long. What I am saying is that there is a deeper well, inside our own hearts, from which we can draw spiritual strength and wisdom that will never leave us empty again.

To drink from this deep fountain of wisdom and love opens up something eternal in us, and empowers us to give life to others.'

'Sir, give me that living water,' the woman begs him eagerly. 'I desire this gift so much, to quench the emptiness inside me, and to be a fountain of life for others. I come here every day and every night, just to get a day's water supply, and my life feels so futile. But what you are saying gives me hope that there is something more than this. And you are saying that the key to that "something" is in my own heart?'

At this point the stranger sends the woman down to the bottom of her personal 'well', knowing that only when she has faced its darkness will she discover the fountain of life she is seeking:

'Go and fetch your husband,' he tells her, 'and come back.'

The woman's face clouds over. The stranger has reached into the most troubled area of her life, and she feels like running away, there and then. Is this the cost of the promised living water? She does not know how to respond. She prevaricates with a half-truth: 'I haven't got a husband.'

'I know,' the stranger tells her, gently. You've been married five times already and your present partner isn't really your husband. You have told the truth.'

The woman is beginning to wish she had never come to the well. She wants to tell this loving, accepting stranger about the pain and the heartache of all those broken relationships, and her feelings of complete failure and breakdown in the face of this trail of devastation in her life. She wants to open up the running sore of her present unhappy partnership, but she dare not show him the murky depths of her heart's well. Instead she tries to change the subject:

'I see you are something of a mind-reader,' she replies. 'Tell me, then: our ancestors regarded this well as sacred ground, but others say you can only find sacred space in a proper church. What do you think?'

The stranger does not challenge her evasion of the burning questions in her life. He knows she has recognized them and that nothing can now stand in the way of her facing and overcoming them, because she has already tasted her first sip of the living water.

He answers her with a gentle smile:

'Believe me, the time will come when we will all come to realize that the whole of creation is sacred ground – wells and churches and cathedrals, no less, and no more than your own back garden. We will learn to read the invisible realities hidden in the visible world in which we live. We will come to trust that each of us carries a seed of God himself in our hearts, and when that seed starts to grow, then nothing is impossible. Implacable enemies become friends and irretrievable breakdowns become new beginnings.'

The woman is speechless. The stranger's words sink deep into her soul and she knows he has told her something profoundly true – something she always knew, but never knew that she knew – something Jacob and all her ancestors knew, but something that might change the bitter cup of her experience into a fountain of new possibility. At last, she answers,

'I know that one day all these things will be true,' she says, 'perhaps in heaven?'

'Heaven is here and now. The secret is in your own heart and your own life, only waiting to open up and grow into fullness.'

The conversation ends there. The man's friends are returning and are more than a little surprised to find him sitting there talking with this woman. For her part, she is so amazed at the sheer power of the encounter, so unexpected, that she goes straight back to the village, leaving her water jar behind her in her haste to tell her neighbours about the man who has seen so deeply into her heart.

It is obvious to them all that something has happened to change her. Something is bubbling out of her, like a fountain. They go back with her, to meet the man who has touched her life so powerfully. They beg him to stay with them, and he stays on for two days, and many people come to hear, and to receive his promise for themselves, because of that chance encounter, at a lonely well, on a hot and dusty day.

Jacob's well, then, has become sacred space for an ordinary woman going about her daily work, and carrying her life's sorrow like a sack of stones around her heart. There she has

been confronted with the real heart of the pain, by one who cares for her more than she cares for herself. And the pain has turned to promise. Circumstances that felt like a tomb, populated only by dead dreams and buried hopes, have been recognized as a womb, from which new life might emerge.

Is it just a fanciful story, or does the stranger know something that you and I know too, deep down in our hearts? Does he have exceptional insight, or is he able to read the woman's invisible, untold story because he gives her his undivided attention and his unconditional love? Is this what can happen where love and imagination meet? Might we all discover that we can meet each other at this deeper, more real level of our being, if we can offer each other the same quality of loving attention?

You might like to spend some time in your personal sacred space, and let this story come alive for you in whatever way it will. Take some time to make your own journey of imagination to the well. Take up your empty water jar and pick your way through the heat and dust of your daily life. See the landscape of your life around you as you trudge through the heat of the day.

Let 'the stranger' approach you and draw you into conversation. Let him (or her) take you to the edge of any 'well' in your own life and show you the truth that lies at the bottom of it. In your imagination, express to the stranger how you really feel about that place of emptiness, or futility, or grief. Let the stranger speak your truth to you in gentle love, and open up new perspectives from which the living water of new possibility might flow. What form might this new possibility take for you? How might you put it into practice? Could you share your story with a trusted friend? Could you be 'the stranger' for someone else?

Whichever way we turn, so it seems, our culture bombards us with reminders of the many, many 'buckets' we are supposed to need, to get enough water from life's well to keep us satisfied and desirable, and well ahead in the race for survival. Every time we watch television or open a glossy magazine, we learn more about the nature of these 'buckets'. They are packed with the latest high-tech gadgets, with products to make us more attractive, with fast cars and fast food and even with those commodities that might please 'the person who has everything'. We are urged to trek to the wells of consumerism every day that we live, to keep ourselves supplied.

The woman at Jacob's well realizes that all these things will never satisfy her deeper longings, but she discovers resources in her own heart which might make the buckets dispensable.

Seasons of turning

Every tree has to let go of its foliage. The autumn tree might also take us further into the pain, and the promise that lies at the bottom of the well and the place of turning. As a way of connecting some of the painful experiences in your life with the fruit that grew from them, you might like to try an exercise along these lines, using whatever materials or images feel right for you.

Imagine your life as an autumn tree. There may have been long, hot summer days, golden with memory, but there may also have been frosts, gales and times of drought. Now, in an autumn season (and seasons like this can arise from time to time, at any age and any period of our lives) you sense a need to let some things go, just as the tree has to let its leaves – and its seeds – fall to the cold, wet earth. At any time in your life, as you stop to reflect, you will find that some of the things you have cherished are dying.

Some of your fallen leaves may represent losses you have suffered through no fault of your own. Others may have resulted from your own wrong choices or actions. Just acknowledge them, without any judgment. Then let yourself notice that along with your fallen leaves there are seeds and fruits falling to the ground.

It may come as a surprise to discover that there is often a direct connection between what has been lost and the new seed that is growing from it. For example, the loss of some particular security may have challenged you beyond your 'comfort zone' and drawn you into an unexpected new level of confidence. These deeper layers of confidence can often only be revealed when an old layer of fear is challenged and confronted. In the same way our genuine doubts about given 'certainties' can be the gateway to deeper levels of truth.

Perhaps a beloved son or daughter has left home to begin an independent life. If you are feeling such a loss, you might like to reflect on the rich new fruit that has been given to the earth in your child's life and all that it will become as it grows freely and independently into fullness. And if your loss is more final than this, and you grieve for a lost loved one, try to give yourself the time and space to reflect on the fruits of that person's life and celebrate them in a way that is meaningful to you, and in a way which helps those fruits to grow for the world your loved one has left.

If a relationship has died in your life, when you feel ready, and strong enough to face your memories, stop to reflect on the difference that relationship has made to both of you while it was still alive, and how those fruits might grow now into something new for each of you and for all creation. Even the most painful relationships are bearing deep fruit, which – if we wish it – can be turned into gifts for ourselves and for others.

The choice is ours – to stay buried in our sorrow at the bottom of the well, or to let the bucket of life draw us back to the waiting world, enriched – not diminished – by our experience of the darkness. If we can make the choice for life, then the bottom of the well will have become sacred space.

Acknowledging our turnings and returnings

Christians might respond to their need for turning (or *metanoia*) by seeking the sacrament of reconciliation. This is a ritualized way of saying, to ourselves, and to God, and perhaps to another human being, 'I recognize something negative or destructive in myself, revealed in my thoughts, words or actions, in this particular issue, and I want to change direction.' Sometimes these 'turnings' are large and dramatic and may change the course of our lives. More often, they arise simply out of the rough and tumble of daily life, and reflect a desire to live more true to the drawing of love and be less driven by our fears and distrusts.

Can you recognize any points of turning in your own life?

- Any major changes of direction that you have made?

- Any smaller shifts of focus you may be aware of, when you have noticed a need to be free of some destructive pattern that may be developing in the way you do or see things?

- Any issues in your life that feel like a dead end, but that you would like to turn into places of new beginning?

Is there any way you would wish to give expression to your desire for a change of direction from negative to positive? For example, can you share your feelings on these matters with a trusted friend? Can you offer a friend the listening space in which to explore such feelings they may be having themselves? Conversations like this can open up those inner resources in each of us that free us from the fears which keep us trekking to the well, and offer us, instead, a source of hope and life that will not dry up, because it comes from the groundwater of our being.

CHAPTER 5

GROVES AND SPRINGS

CIRCLES OF HOSPITALITY

Wells have to be dug. They cost us effort and heartache. To reach the water of life they might yield, we have to delve deep into ourselves, and descend through dark, and sometimes fearful, shafts before we reach the point of turning, and returning.

Springs are a different kind of sacred space. There is a spontaneity in the image of the spring – something that rises up, giving pure water without our effort. Spring water is given to us gratuitously. It bubbles up from the depths of the earth without our doing and supplies energy and life without our asking. It trickles, uninvited, from cracks in the hard rock of our experience. It takes us by surprise, appearing out of nowhere to refresh and encourage us.

Springs are often found among woodland, watering the

growth of the surrounding trees. Sheltering groves grow up around a source of spring water, as if the trees were gathering to pay their respects to what gives them life. Such places are sacred space in the Celtic vision, and our fifth station brings us into the restfulness and the refreshment of our inner groves and springs. Here we shall draw deeply on the hospitality these blessed circles offer us, pausing to receive the gift of their communion, before moving on.

The groves of companionship

We speak of our 'circle of friends', and it is this intimate inner circle of our lives that can perhaps lead us most readily into the sacred groves of our innermost hearts. You might like to pause for a few minutes and reflect on your own 'circle'. Who is included in it? What are their names? What do you especially value about each of these friends? What do you think each of them especially values about *you*? Just allow the unique gifts of every individual in your circle to be brought to mind. Let it be like a shared meal, to which each of you is bringing his or her own particular contribution. This is the feast you are invited to celebrate in the sacred grove of this 'station'. It is a communion meal, with the power not only to nourish you, but also to transform you.

So the 'trees' in our inner sacred groves are the people around us – our circle of friends, our immediate family, our colleagues and fellow workers, our neighbours and those with whom we share our lives in any way. Most of us have an inner circle of people who are deeply trusted and loved, and beyond that there will be outer circles of people with whom we are thrown together by circumstance, or with whom we choose – or are forced – to spend some of our time. For the Celts the circle would have been wider still, including, as it might for us too, those 'wisdom figures' who have gone ahead of us – our ancestors, and our saints and angels, both those who are universally acknowledged and those known only to ourselves.

Whoever they are, and however we feel about them individually, all the people in our grove have roots and branches, like the woodland trees, and each of them has a personal identity, just as an oak is not a beech tree, nor a rowan tree a bramble bush. For the most part, at least in the early stages of any relationship, we tend to meet each other in 'the branches' of our experience, that is, in the outward and visible things we share. We see each other as physical beings, with particular characteristics and our own style of doing things. We learn to recognize each other's likes and dislikes. We are invited into each other's homes, perhaps. Our 'above-ground' lives form part of the human forest, maybe fighting for space to become who we really are, maybe entangled with each other in joyful harmony or terrible knots.

I remember especially a tree I noticed once on a country lane in Wales. One of its branches had been almost severed, either by storm or sickness. It had broken away from the trunk and fallen across a branch of a neighbouring tree. This neighbouring branch had broken its fall and continued to hold it in its half-severed state, probably through many years. As I watched, I could hear the supporting tree branch creaking under the weight of its broken neighbour. Perhaps some of our 'branch' encounters are like that – we may feel oppressed by the burden of another human life that weighs upon us and depends on us for support. Or we may ourselves be in need of that kind of holding. Either way, the trees can teach us something of what *communion* might mean.

The Celts, however, would have been quick to recall that in all things there is an invisible, as well as a visible, dimension, and the space where the invisible becomes manifest in the visible is sacred. If we look below the surface of our human circles, we become aware that what we experience in our relationships with our companions is profoundly shaped by a vast invisible network of roots we cannot see. As friendship deepens into genuine intimacy, we begin to understand a little of the nature of the other person's 'roots'. This may radically alter our perceptions. To know something of a person's history, of what makes them 'come alive' and what 'deadens' them, or of the difficulties they have grown through, is to understand them at a much deeper level. The more we know of this invisible reality of each other, the more

we understand, and the more we understand, the more readily we can forgive whatever needs to be forgiven.

Every individual in our personal sacred grove – and indeed in all of creation – is a sacred space, where the invisible of all that makes them who they are is expressed in the visible person we encounter. How might we revere the sacredness of each other? Perhaps by making a more conscious effort to tell them of the particular ways in which we value them (and there is something to value even in the people who cause us the most heartache, if we take the time and trouble to search a little). In what ways do we diminish the value of others and demean their personalities? Do we try to build up our own self-esteem by shrinking theirs? Do we tend to criticize more readily than we praise them? The hospitality of the sacred grove asks us to enter each other's space respectfully, gently and lovingly. Without this reverence there can be no communion.

Pause for a while to reflect on one or two people in your own circle of friends – perhaps one person you are especially close to, and another with whom you feel less at ease. If you could imagine these people as trees, with roots and branches, how would you describe their branches – their visible lives and personalities? What do you know of their roots – their invisible reality – and how they have been shaped by their personal stories and the way their lives have unfolded? If you feel able to do so, perhaps make an effort to discover a little more about the roots of the people you have chosen. Does this make any difference to the way you relate to them?

When we recognize the importance of our own invisible roots, and respect that of others, we are moving into common ground, where real communion of heart and mind might become a possibility.

Cultivating common ground

Wherever you live, there is sure to be a place, or several places, where people gather together. In our village the children tend to flock to a grassy bank by the village pool where there are some swings, and the young people congregate by the bridge. Older people regularly meet on Thursdays at the Post Office when they collect their pensions. It's a familiar pattern. So familiar that we don't even think about it. Yet it is so fundamental to our way of being human that our language has a word for it. We call it 'common ground'. For our Celtic pilgrimage, this kind of common ground is an important signpost to the sacred groves of companionship.

Its opposite is the kind of land we describe as 'no man's land'. Between hostile territories this might take the form of a strip of land going right along the border, stripped of all its trees and bushes and living things, and seeded instead with mines which will kill any living thing that tries to cross it. Human conflict and human fear turn this dead land into a death-land.

Common ground *attracts* people, draws them into community, and includes all comers. The village fairground doesn't question our origins or our qualifications. It just lets us be there, and welcomes us; makes us feel at home. It engenders happiness and a sense of security. It helps to melt our hesitant aloneness into a confident togetherness.

A no man's land does the opposite. It *repels* us. It creates a barrier. It causes grief. It feeds on fear. It turns our bedrock togetherness into frightened isolation. Such places can be found in our cities, and in ourselves and our relationships. Do we want them to be there? Can we do anything to change the no man's land to common ground?

One way to reclaim no man's land and turn it gradually back into common ground is to practise the art of relating to others in the roots of our being, rather than merely in our outermost branches.

No man's land rears its head, for example, when topics are touched upon in conversation that cause hackles to rise. Sometimes it is almost possible to watch people's defence systems coming into operation. Once this has happened, there is unlikely to be any further fruitful interchange. The people concerned will probably switch the conversation to something non-controversial, like the weather. The conversation might continue, but it will have been 'rendered harmless' by bringing it up to a more superficial level, where those concerned unconsciously agree not to offend or be offended.

With a bit of goodwill, however, common ground might be discovered. Take, for example, two people who are colleagues, with very little in common except the place where they happen to work. They fall out very easily, each having different ideas about how things should be done. When these differences come to the surface, they 'freeze' each other into a no man's land of non-communication – because they cannot speak about the matter in hand without quarrelling, they maintain only the minimum contact necessary for courtesy, with polite exchanges about the weather or the shops or the cinema. One day, however, they discover a shared and passionate commitment to ecology (for example) and the desire to save endangered species.

Once they become aware of this 'common ground', they know that however badly they may fall out about 'less important' matters, they have this deep connectedness. If they are wise they will remember this, and when the sparks begin to fly, they will bear in mind that what connects them is more real, more permanent, more important and more life-giving than what divides them. This may not reduce the frequency of their disagreements, but it will take the sting out of them and base their relationship on a much sounder footing.

And what is true for individuals is true for whole communities. In strife-torn lands entire physical areas can be turned into 'no man's land', alongside an adamant refusal to discuss differences peacefully: 'We cannot agree therefore we will not talk.' A search for common ground, on the other hand, has inspired countless individuals and communities in such situations to become quiet witnesses of reconciliation and life.

Now go back to your own sacred grove of friends, colleagues and companions, and notice the ground it grows on. Is there any no man's land? Are you happy with the amount of common ground you share, or would you like to extend it?

Most of the tension in life arises in our relationships with those who are closest to us – partners, families and colleagues. Look at one or two of the most significant relationships in your life. Can you see the 'common ground' that connects you? Can you think of ways to foster it and let it become a healer of tension?

Think of one or two people you absolutely cannot get on with. Can you discover any common ground at all between you – perhaps a shared interest, or something common in your background? To discover common ground, you have to go 'deep'. This means taking the risk of a snub, or worse, approaching the disliked person in openness and friendship and making yourself vulnerable. But the rewards may surprise you. The person you are avoiding may be very frightened inside, and may come more than halfway to meet you if you genuinely mean well.

Common ground is the only place in which genuine communion can be experienced. It allows both our visible and our invisible realities to be respected and given space to grow, and it is the place where we begin to realize we are truly all one below the tideline.

The gift of our sacred groves is to bind us together into human communities, large and small, and just as towns and villages evolve around a source of water, or other resources essential to life, so our personal groves evolve around a 'spring'. The springs that water our communities come in many different forms. Perhaps we bond with certain people because of a shared joy in some sport or hobby, or, quite commonly, through the pain of a shared difficulty. Perhaps our 'spring' is the common ground of children in the same age group or at the same school. Perhaps a shared passion for some political, social or spiritual ideal draws us together. You might like to reflect for a moment on your own personal groves, and on the springs that feed them and give them life.

● What 'springs' supply energy to you personally, or to any group of people in which you feel at home? They may be memories, experiences or particular relationships that give you life, for example. How have they inspired your onward journey?

• Have you ever been aware of discovering a 'spring' of life-giving energy in your life? This might have taken you by surprise – flowing from people or events you would never have expected to be so life-giving. New and positive energy may even have sprung out of people or situations you would have preferred to avoid at the time. Sometimes what seemed like a 'well' can become a 'spring'.

• And because, in the bedrock, we are all one, how can our lives become living springs of creative energy for others?

If we look carefully, and travel expectantly, we will often find little springs of life simply in our routine living. A very worthwhile exercise is to look back over each day – just for a minute or two, perhaps before falling asleep – and notice anything in the day's events that gave you new energy or inspired you.

And what about the sacred springs that provide our personal flow of energy? The book of Genesis paints an imaginative picture of God's first Dream of creation, and calls it the Garden of Eden. In the middle of this garden it envisages a spring of fresh water, flowing out over all the surrounding earth. Before anything grew on Earth, or any life evolved, this first primeval spring flowed forth.

This same spring of primeval creative energy wells up in every creature. It may become apparent in many different ways, each of them potentially creative and generative of new life and vision. Our own deep springs of creative energy may become visible, for example, in sexual desire, parental nurturing, artistic inspiration, campaigning vigour, compassionate caring, or sheer persistence in the face of hardship. These are a few of their visible manifestations, but in their invisible reality they are all expressions of the one source of creative life springing from the heart of all creation and manifesting itself in an infinite variety of

forms. How do you feel you are expressing your own creativity? How are you generating new life in your own personal way? In what particular ways is that first primeval spring of energy flowing out in your life?

Twelve springs and seventy palm trees

If you have ever been in a desert region you will be especially aware of how life gathers instinctively around the source of water. Today, in the Western world at least, there are few deserts and our water comes to us through the mains-supply lines. But we know different deserts. We know the emotional deserts of loneliness and alienation from each other, deserts of fear, anxiety or despair, and the aridity of lives untouched by love. Almost all of us, at some time in our lives, will have experienced the desert in this way and for some of us it will seem to be our permanent place of existence. The Jesus of the Christian gospel said he had come to bring life, and life in all its fullness. Can there be hope of such life in our deserts?

The sacred groves, fed by sacred springs, encourage us to search for life. And those who have walked the desert ways before us share their wisdom with us as we grope our way forward. In the book of Exodus (chapter 16) we find a band of desert travellers who discover a circle of hospitality in a hostile environment, and learn to understand its challenges. We might listen in to a little of their story as they encamp in the deserts of Sinai:

Times had been spectacularly difficult for the children of Israel. A dramatic escape from slavery in Egypt, initiated and guided by their leader Moses, had eventually brought them to relative – though very uncomfortable – freedom as they trekked across the desert in the perennial human search for a place they could call 'home'. The pattern of their lives had fallen into the simple rhythm of walking until they found food and water, and then encamping at that place, before moving on again, their strength temporarily renewed.

We find them, first, at a place called Marah. There was

water here and they fell upon it eagerly, only to discover that it was polluted and undrinkable. They turned on their leader and complained. 'How are we supposed to drink this bitter water?' they demanded. Moses, not for the first time, had no answer to their complaining, but turned, in his own helplessness, to appeal to God for help. The answer came in the shape of a piece of wood which, when thrown into the polluted water, made it pure again and fit to drink. The water, thus cleansed, clearly gave them the strength they needed to walk a little further, until they came to Elim where they found twelve springs and seventy palm trees, and there they pitched camp beside the water.

Having found this place of natural hospitality, offering shelter and water, the weary travellers now needed food, and again they came to Moses with their complaints. 'Why did you bring us out here?' they railed. 'If we have only come out here to die of starvation in the desert, we might as well have stayed in slavery in Egypt, where at least our oppressors fed us.' But God was ready with another miracle, in response to the pleadings of the desperate Moses. 'I shall rain down bread from heaven,' God promised, 'and all you need to do is collect it.' And so it happened that the desert itself provided a meal for its unhappy guests. Not just for a day, but for forty years, as long as their wanderings continued. Quails, migrating across the Mediterranean from Europe, fell, exhausted from their flight, in large numbers, providing meat for the travellers, and a bread-like substance called manna, secreted by insects living on the tamarisk trees, was there for the gathering every dawn.

The trek continued on its weary, but determined trail, and again the water ran out. Moses was once more called to account, and appealed to God for help. 'How am I to deal with these wayward people?' he pleaded. 'Any minute now they will start to stone me if they don't find any water.' And once more God revealed an unexpected source of life. 'Take your staff,' he directed Moses, 'and strike it against that rock over there.' Moses did as he was told. He took his staff and struck against the hard desert rock, and a spring of fresh water was released.

This little episode from the annals of a journey far distant from our own can perhaps help us to discover our own desert home with its twelve springs and seventy palm trees. At the very least it can teach us some desert wisdom:

- Water can be polluted and unfit to drink. We all know that this is true physically, but what of our spiritual 'water supplies'. Perhaps we feel that much of what invades our living rooms via the mass media today, and even some of what is imposed upon us by the various 'teaching authorities' in our world, is not a source of life, but is infecting us, and our world, with bitterness and discontentment. If so, are we able ourselves to inject new life and more human values into our environment? What 'sticks' are available to us personally, to regenerate the stale spiritual waters of our times? They may be nothing more dramatic than a readiness to speak an affirming word instead of a word of complaint, or the courage to speak out truth when it would be more comfortable to collude with the lies.

- A source of life can sometimes be found in the hard rock of our experience. Our instinct is to shun the hard rock of life and dismiss it as a no-go area, yet Moses was directed to face the hard rock head-on and trust that in its depths there would be a source of new life, just as there can be treasure at the bottom of our wells and seams of gold from our broken lightning. Is there some hard rock around for us right now? Can we risk looking it in the face, to recognize what it is giving to us, in the currency of wisdom and insight, for the way ahead?

- The desert of experience can give us unexpected nourishment. The lesson of the manna and the quails, however, reveals he need to live one day at a time. The manna could not be stored. Those who tried to take more than they needed, to save themselves a job the next morning, found the manna had 'gone off' overnight and was uneatable. The quails were a seasonal meal. The travellers through the desert had to come to terms with the fact that everything is *provisional*.

'Provisional' means two things – it is impermanent, yet it *provides*. Desert wisdom tells us we must trust the day, take and receive its gifts, but not cling to them for ourselves. Desert hospitality is about the receiving, and the sharing, of life's 'provisions', taking only what we need, and entrusting tomorrow into the hands that gave us today.

When this kind of wisdom becomes embedded in our hearts, we can turn the dream of twelve springs and seventy palm trees into a reality, for ourselves and for each other.

You might like to pause awhile and reflect on how you see your own life's journey. Have there been desert times and places? What has sustained life in you in such times? What has kept you going? It may have been the encouragement of particular people. If so, can you tell them what they have meant to you? Or perhaps you are enlivened and encouraged by a particular community or circle to which you belong. Notice and celebrate that circle thankfully, and maybe ponder on how it might become even more open and welcoming, as an oasis for others. What brings life into your family? How can you encourage it? What tends to 'pollute' the atmosphere in your home? Can you do anything to free yourself of the source of pollution? Your own participation in any community, large or small, makes a difference to that community. Do you feel that you are bringing life to those you spend time with, or does your presence dampen their energy? Don't judge yourself, but simply be aware, as honestly as you can, of what is happening in your own circles of hospitality, and reflect on how you might wish to make any small but positive changes.

I once made a desert walk in Sinai myself, among a group of pilgrims led by a Bedouin guide, to ascend Mount Sinai to see the sunrise from the summit. We set out in the middle of the night, beneath a brilliant star-laden sky. For the few hours it took to reach the mountain and climb its lower reaches, the group of walkers, from many different nations and cultures, and all strangers to each other, bickered and groused as vehemently as Moses' little party. For some the pace was too slow, for others too fast. Some wanted to stop and rest, others couldn't move forward fast enough. Some disapproved of the way the guide was leading us, and fell out with every stone along the way. Others were content just to fall out with each other over any pretext that came to hand.

It was a thoroughly ragged band of sinners who reached the summit of Sinai that morning, and it has to be said that even the glory of the desert sunrise failed to bond us into any kind of genuine fellowship, as we persisted in getting in the way of each other's photography. We began the descent. The sun rose and so did the temperature. Soon we were streaming with sweat and desperate for water. Some of the pilgrims had brought plenty of water with them. Others had not been so careful in their preparations. A remarkable truce broke out. Those without water stopped complaining and began to make friends with those who had water. Those with the water, on the whole, were sorry for those who had not, and so the water bottles were passed round and shared. Hardship had forged communion where all else had failed. We found water in a hard rock, and the stick of our common humanity eventually turned our grouses into gestures of friendship.

Halfway down the mountain we found our manna and quails, in the shape of a solitary Bedouin shepherd who had a small campfire going, near a clump of thorn bushes, and was brewing a wonderful aromatic tea, which he gladly shared with us all. It tasted, truly, like manna from heaven, and came to us just as unexpectedly and undeservedly. The Bedouin smiled, quietly, out of the deep calm of his presence and his trust in the mountain that sustained him. He gave each of us a draught of desert wisdom in those little beakers of tea that morning as he drew the circle of real communion around our ragged edges.

Breaking bread

A draught of wisdom was the very last thing that two weary and disappointed travellers were expecting one afternoon, 2,000 years ago, as they trudged along the road from Jerusalem to Emmaus. We read their story in Luke's Gospel (chapter 24):

Like their forebears in the desert, these travellers were traumatized
by events that had unfolded in their lives and the lives of their
people. A friend of theirs had just been executed. Well he was more
than a friend, because they had been sure he was going to be the
one to set Israel free from the bondage of Roman rule, and they had
thrown their lot in with him completely. And now he was dead and
buried, and their hopes and dreams were buried along with him. As
they walked, they talked over all that had happened.

Eventually a stranger came up behind them. They were
aware of his approaching footsteps, and expected him to overtake
them. Instead he fell in alongside them and matched his pace to
theirs. In a friendly, non-threatening tone, he asked, 'What are you
discussing so solemnly, as you walk along?'

'You must be the only one for miles around who hasn't heard
all that has been happening in Jerusalem this week!' they retorted.

'Tell me more,' he invited them.

'Haven't you heard about Jesus of Nazareth, whom everyone
recognized as a prophet and a healer and the bringer of new hope
for Israel? And how the leaders of our church and state couldn't
cope with everything he stood for, and had him done to death? We
were so sure he would be the one to set Israel free. And that's not
all. There's a rumour going round that some women from our
group went to his tomb early this morning, and when they couldn't
find his body there, they saw a vision of angels who told them he is
still alive! But none of us has seen him.'

The stranger listened to their story with rapt attention, and
then mused quietly for a while, before answering them: 'Suppose
this friend of yours really was the one to free Israel – isn't this just
what the prophets said must happen before his reign could begin
and his kingdom come? Just listen. The pattern is all there, revealed
in the story of Israel and in the story of the whole human family.'

And the stranger went on to tell them, in a fresh and vivid
way, their own story. How humanity had made its own bid for
autonomy and lost its connectedness with God. How humankind had
thus set out on a pilgrimage of life that would take them beyond the
slavery of their own compulsions and power struggles, always moving

on to something beyond themselves, always longing for 'the place
of resurrection', and their eternal home. And how that place of
resurrection would be discovered only by passing through the eye
of a needle – through the dereliction of the 'place of poverty', the
bottom of the well, the apparent death of every hope and dream.

It felt like a fire being kindled in their hearts and memories
as the stranger spoke.

At last they came to a crossroads,
and the stranger made to walk on. They
intended to stop at a roadside inn and
have a meal, and they begged him to
join them. Only three days earlier they
had shared a last meal with their friend.
The poignancy of the connection struck
new sorrow into them as they began
their meal. Then the stranger picked up
a piece of bread, offered thanks, and
broke it into three, giving each of them a
piece. He looked into their eyes, and the
moment became charged with a whole
new vision, as if he had dissolved the
scales from their eyes. And in that
moment they knew the truth of what the
women had seen that morning. In the
breaking of the bread they knew the

hopes and dreams that had died – God's own Dream for creation –
were alive, were with them now, and would live for ever.

Passing through

This story is a powerful reminder that the human traveller is a
'guest of the world'. In the Celtic vision, we are strangers passing
through God's creation, yet each with the power to affect that
creation either for better or for worse. Every individual makes a
difference. It is our own choice as to what that difference shall
be – either creative or destructive.

In the Christian service of holy communion, the bread that

is broken and shared is often called 'the host'. This reminds us that creation, and its creator, are our hosts as we spend our lives in privileged and sacred time as guests of the Earth. This reality came vividly to life for me one year when I was spending some time with friends in their countryside home. You might like to join me in my musings as I woke up one lovely summer morning.

Everything was completely silent in the little garden bungalow as I opened my eyes tentatively, dreamily, to the dawn of another shimmering morning. The sun was already clamouring at the bedroom window, and the freckled shadows of the hazelnut tree were dappling the fresh white net curtains with all the insistence of summer green. I lay perfectly still, not stirring an inch from where I was lying when I woke, simply relishing this time of quiet and perfect enjoyment of a new morning. My eyes rested on the neatly finished corner of the papered, whitewashed wall, where it met the dark pine of the window sill. Through the open window I could hear the hungry demands of the thrush chicks and the little greenfinch family. Beyond the hazelnuts, the sunflowers stretched their dinner-plate faces to the eastern light in a sumptuous surrender to the warming and the glory of the day, and greeted their towering hollyhock neighbours, gentle giants among the tomatoes and cucumbers, the dill and the dahlias and the beans.

I felt so completely a part of the new awakening day that this moment could have lasted for ever, and all would have been well. The light of dawn felt like the light of the world. Just as the previous night, in my friends' garden, the immediate, compelling presence of the full moon had enthralled me.

I was a guest in this bungalow. A visitor, passing through. My hosts were sleeping in the next room, or perhaps already preparing breakfast, or walking to the baker's for the morning rolls. My hosts. Yet there was a larger presence – infinitely large – a 'forever-host'. I had seen its icon in the sky by night, symbol of an eternal presence held in the star-studded expanse of the night skies. I had felt its power in the new awakening day beyond the window.

It led me to reflect that I am passing through a world I did not create, just as I was passing through this garden and this bungalow my friends had created. I am here by divine invitation, a guest in this world. Its creator did not have to invite me in. I never asked. He must have wanted me to come. He must have prepared for my coming, at least as lovingly as these, my earthly hosts, had prepared for my visit. He must have dreamed of all that we would do, and discover, together, long before I arrived.

I lay there, looking round the contents of the room, the pictures on the wall, the photographs and souvenirs of this and that. What I saw told me so much about my hosts. From all I saw and experienced in their home, I discovered aspects of their personal reality. I could see their image imprinted upon all they had created and established and arranged. And I felt their love for me in all the little touches of beautiful, unnecessary hospitality they had devised to make me feel welcome and at home.

It made me realize what the forever-host is doing in his world for us, his beloved guests. It made me present to creation in a different, more vibrant way. I began to realize that for our short stay on this Earth, we ourselves become a part of how God is expressing his eternal reality in the created world. We are the pictures on his wall, fireflies in the night reflecting his silver moonlight. He is calling us to express a fragment of his nature to others passing through, just as they express their own fragments of him to us.

Every new day calls us into life. We have to rise. Up into the bright, white, green-dappled, blue-streaked morning. We have to let the Earth turn once more about its axis so that the new day can reveal its own new secrets and draw its own new lines and colours in the image of its maker. As I rose that morning, I understood more deeply what the Celts knew intuitively, that in every experience of life we can discover the brushstrokes of God's self-portrait and we ourselves become part of his self-disclosure.

Seasons of companionship

Our sacred groves are signs and sacraments of this eternal hospitality – offered *to* us by our circle of friends and companions, and offered *by* us to all whose need we become aware of. Seasons of companionship run through our lives like golden threads, and there is no time of life in which we do not yearn for the intimacy of true friendship and a sense of belonging.

We find this intimacy as we gather round the particular springs of sacred energy that bring us to life and nourish our continuing growth into who we really are. They keep us alive in our desert wanderings, and they refresh our fruitfulness.

Once, while visiting a medieval cathedral, I lingered at the west door, examining the ancient sanctuary knocker, and reading the description of what happened to a fugitive who claimed sanctuary there. Three things were offered to such a person:

● A place of safety where he could sleep;

● Food to keep him alive;

● Time in which to reflect on what he was doing and what he would do in the future.

It struck me that these three things are very similar to what we offer each other in our sacred groves – safe space, nourishment, both physical and spiritual, and time to reflect on who we are and what we desire. We give each other safe space when we listen to each other's deep-felt experience, with respect and without judgment. We nourish each other when we share our 'common ground', and when we give each other the warmth of encouragement and affirmation and the sunlight of positive regard and genuine affection. We give each other time for becoming who we really are, when we acknowledge that none of us is a finished product, and the growth and maturing of each of us is being profoundly affected by the attitudes of all of us.

And where we receive these gifts is a place we can truly call 'home'.

Daily bread – everyday bread

Sometimes God's self-disclosure catches us unawares, and we gasp in awe at its sudden revelation. The two travellers in the Emmaus story shared a communion meal with the stranger, and it was a communion which was to transform their way of seeing things from that moment on. God himself 'passed through' their immediate experience, and transformed it. And they were then called to carry the presence of that heart knowledge of God through the world for as long as they remained its guests. We too are called to carry the spark of eternity with us on our journey through creation and to kindle more and more of the fire of God by touching all creation and all creatures with love. This is the effect of every true communion we share.

The word 'communion' means a coming together 'as one'. This is, ultimately, what makes the groves of our friendships sacred. The word 'companion' means 'one with whom bread is shared'. A holy communion meal, as celebrated sacramentally by Christians, is a meal in which people come together as one to share sacred bread. It is a celebration of the potential in humankind to be transformed into a new and eternal reality, which nevertheless begins here on Earth in our own homes and cities.

Sadly, our 'union' is often more symbolic than effective, but the *desire* for real human communion, however we might wish to express that communion, is the first beginning of its own fulfilment. In looking for genuine communion and companionship with each other we are making a statement that we know, deep down, we are one, in the mystery embodied in the infinite knot, and we wish our lives could show forth more of that deep-down oneness.

The 'bread' we share in the circle of our own sacred groves is the bread of our own lives and the chalice contains the wine of our own joys and sorrows. In a communion meal, we pass the bread from hand to hand, each taking a fragment, just as a family might pass the bread basket round the kitchen table. We pass the wine to each other, as friends might share intimate moments of joy or of grief in each other's company, holding what is shared in sacred trust.

For the Celtic spirit the bread of our daily lives is as sacred as the consecrated host in a communion service. The wine of our daily joy and sorrow is to be revered as deeply as the wine in the communion chalice. Life itself, wherever we are living it out in practice and in fact, is our communion table. How do we handle the bread of each other's lives? How freely do we share our own? I am told there are human communities in which the custom is not to eat any of the bread fetched fresh from the baker's until a part of it has been given away to someone in need. To share our daily lives is to give freely, to those who need them, our minutes and our hours, our help, our expertise, our compassion and our love, as well as our material resources. A community where such a spirit of sharing is second nature would be a sacred grove indeed.

'We are one'

'Communion', however we might choose to express it, asserts and affirms the deep truth that in the heart of creation 'we are one'. We need to return, over and over again, to the awareness of the bedrock unity that is discovered below the tideline of our everyday consciousness. A little exercise helps me to return to this awareness from time to time:

● Bring your two hands together slowly, allowing only the fingertips to touch at first. This level of connection is a reflection of the everyday interactions we have with each other. Our individual lives remain separate entities, like the two hands, but there is some 'fingertip contact' in our dealings with each other.

- Now press your fingers closer together and allow them to touch all the way down, joint by joint, till you reach your knuckles. This takes much more effort. Indeed, it can create tension and make your hands feel tired. Learning to come closer to each other can also be difficult and demanding. The two hands want to spring away from each other and be their separate selves.

- Finally, allow your two hands to come together completely, like a child in prayer, until your palms are flat against each other. The tension has gone now and the position feels more natural. There is even a feeling of each hand supporting the other. Your hands are still two separate parts of your body, but they have come together in a gesture of oneness. At this point it becomes very obvious that they are two parts of *one* body.

When I take a moment to do this little exercise, I sometimes let my hands represent myself and someone from whom I am separated, or perhaps someone I find difficult. At first we are far apart, or possibly touching each other only superficially, but as the exercise deepens, I realize that in the bedrock, *we are one*.

You might like to take this exercise one step further. When your hands have come together as one, transfer the pressure to your wrists, and let your hands spread out again, joined at the wrist, but open in a gesture of offering. This is the point where our realization of our bedrock oneness can move on to become a genuine sharing and giving of the bread and wine of our own lives to our grove companions and to all the hungry world.

Whether you belong to a particular faith community or not, and whatever form your personal groves and springs may take, you are sharing in a holy communion every time you recognize your deep kinship with another human heart.

Encouraged, nourished, strengthened, and in some degree transformed by this communion we share in our sacred circles of hospitality, we move on in our pilgrimage, ready to face new thresholds of challenge and change.

CHAPTER 6

CROSSING PLACES

THRESHOLDS OF GROWTH

When I think back to the day I first left home, at the age of nineteen, to live overseas, something heaves inside me. I close my eyes and I can still see the familiar landmarks of my home town drifting past the window as the train gathered speed, and still feel the sick weight of knowing I would never live there again. Even more poignantly, I can still see the outline of my parents, standing on the platform, waving goodbye, as their only chick flew the nest. Seasons of 'at-home-ness' give way to seasons of moving on, of crossing new thresholds.

Whenever I go to Liverpool I stop for a few moments' reflection in the shadow of the famous 'Liver Bird' – symbol of the spirit of that city, and surely the last thing so many emigrants would have seen of a beloved homeland, as their boats left

Liverpool Docks for the New World. Many people have their own memories of such icons of transition – the white cliffs of Dover, the Statue of Liberty or perhaps just the garden gate of a childhood home, loved, left, but never forgotten.

The Celtic vision reveres crossing places and thresholds of all kinds as sacred space. In our inner worlds such places may offer ways across chasms of fear, solid ground through seas of doubt and uncertainty, and openings into new stages of becoming who we really are. Three symbols of transition are especially potent:

- *Bridges and gateways* express a determined refusal to be stopped by what blocks our way. Bridges cross rivers and chasms in the physical landscape. They reconnect what is divided. Gateways open up new paths for us and invite us to enter.

- *Causeways* open up pathways to places that have been inaccessible. Geographically, causeways often provide the means of travelling to tidal islands. On our inner pilgrimage they might be invitations to move forward towards what is new and unknown. They expose the bedrock of a deeper security than the provisional safe places we have to leave behind.

- *Burial grounds* mark the crossing place from life to death, from 'this world' to an 'other world', from time and space to eternity and infinity. We may remember our dead in the calm of a rural churchyard, or in the memorial places to the victims of mass terror. Inwardly, we may find sacred space in the very places where we thought we had buried our dreams.

Here, at the sixth station of our Celtic pilgrimage, we stop to reflect on the crossing places in our own experience – those we have already encountered and passed through, perhaps, and those we may be facing even now, or approaching with apprehension in the future. We might reflect especially on three particular ways in which we are challenged to cross into unknown territory:

- When we come up against resistance along the path we had intended to take, or against emotional blocks that can either push us over the edge into despair, or invite us to take the risk of breaking through the barriers in our lives;

- When we are pitched into a new and possibly frightening stage of our lives, or challenging new demands, and feel we have lost all control over what we are doing and where we are going;

- When we face our own mortality, including the death of our dreams, and stand in the burial ground of all we had hoped for, wondering, 'Is this all there is?'

None of these spaces is where any of us would freely choose to find ourselves. Yet each of them is a crossing place. On the Celtic Way, each of them is sacred space.

Crossing the waters of life

Not surprisingly, given the coastal location of the Celtic regions, in Britain and Ireland at least, the spirit of the sea is central to the Celtic vision of life. Crossing an expanse of water is often not only a daily necessity, but also a sacred act, symbolically taking the traveller from known and familiar territory to what is still unknown and challenging.

To set out to cross water is to relinquish the security of home ground and the sacred sense of place, and entrust oneself to where there is 'no place', and where we are stripped of our own resources. Pilgrimage, whether it takes the form of an actual journey, or an inward one, will always lead us to those moments or stages in our lives when we have to surrender something of the securities of the past, and step out into something new.

Our instinctive reaction to the loss of security in our lives is to look for ways of crossing the uncertainty:

- For bridges *over* the troubled waters or for boats that will carry us safely across the surging seas, or;

• For solid ground *below* the waters of life. This is the kind of solid ground we find in a causeway, or a ford, where the bedrock is revealed below the waters of our lives' turbulence and flux, giving us safe passage to the next stage of our journey.

Sometimes the crossing places that present themselves are trustworthy; sometimes not. How can we learn to tell the difference?

Solid ground or false floors?

An image lingers in my memory from a television news report about torrential flooding, caused by freak storms, in a region where this was extremely unusual. People had been literally swept out of their homes, and their streets had turned overnight into rivers. The TV pictures showed the emergency services struggling to rescue those trapped in upper storeys of their homes, or floating in makeshift boats along their high streets.

Then the focus of the report changed. A reporter was interviewing a couple who had found an ingenious way to solve the problem for themselves. They had seen the waters rising, and had moved themselves and their most valued furniture upstairs. There, they had constructed a false floor, several feet above the level of the real one. They had installed themselves on this false floor, which they hoped would keep them dry until the flood waters receded, and they sat there with the reporter, commenting on their feelings about the situation.

I had to admire their ingenuity. But it was impossible not to feel uneasy about the possibility of sitting high and dry on a false floor, while all around were in great distress. It made me reflect, uncomfortably, about the tendency in all of us to install 'false floors' to keep us safe, and to tempt us into ignoring the realities going on underneath the floorboards.

A political way of making a false floor, for example, might be to suggest that one particular sub-group of the population is threatening our communal security, to isolate that sub-group, and even to try to eliminate it. Such elimination does not have to mean extermination camps or ethnic cleansing in the way we generally understand it. It can mean undermining the self-esteem of particular groupings of people to the extent that they

no longer feel fully human. This can happen in our neighbourhoods, as well as in our dictatorships.

Socially, we make false floors when we draw lines below what we find acceptable, and refuse to think about anything which falls below that line. This 'anything' might include the homeless, the jobless, the prisoners, the very young, the very old, those whose sexual orientation differs from our own, or any with handicaps or difficulties that we would prefer not to face.

In religious institutions, false floors often appear in the form of absolute dogmatism, telling us exactly what we have to believe, what we may or may not discuss, and expelling us from membership if we fail to comply. False floors like these range from 'absolute' statements on how the church is to be run, to 'absolute' statements on how God created the world, and how long it took him.

And what of the false floors we make in our own personal lives, to keep our feet dry in the flood of life? They can be much harder to recognize. We may install ourselves for long periods on 'floors' that feel very solid, such as particular friendships and relationships, family support systems, jobs and careers, a particular lifestyle, or a pattern of achievement in some field of activity, or even our own continuing good health. We don't realize that these securities were not as secure as we thought, until they let us down. And what then? The temptation is to rebuild another false floor. We look for something else that will make us feel safe. We rush into another relationship, or we strive to find another way of feeling that we matter. To face the abyss that seems to be opening up beneath us feels unthinkable. But suppose there were a new depth of solid ground *underneath* the security we have lost. Suppose this new solid ground were more trustworthy than the old.

A baby in the womb could show us how true this is. For the unborn child, the mother's womb is the total story of what it means to be secure. But the time comes when this security is shattered, and the baby plunges into the birth canal, to be expelled, as it seems, into a hostile new environment. We know, of course, that for most babies this new environment is not inherently hostile, and that birth is in fact the gateway to a new way of life, a new level of security. But the baby has no such understanding. Small wonder that he usually arrives screaming! Not surprisingly, her first act in the new world is to seek out, instinctively, the replacement security of her mother's breast.

And so it goes on. Life strips us, over and over, of securities we have actually *outgrown*, but cannot imagine living without, just as a seed is stripped of its husk to allow a new season's growth to happen. At the other end of life, I have seen people whose lives have been very fruitful, and crowned with achievement, having to let go of health, mental clarity and much material comfort as they have made their final journey towards death. Yet some of those people have grown enormously in spiritual stature, as they have embraced the losses, to receive, with empty hands, the treasure of a much deeper sense of the true ground of their being.

We sometimes punish our wayward teenagers by 'grounding' them, that is, by refusing them permission to go out with their friends for a certain period of time. The word 'grounding' has come to mean something negative and punitive, and limiting of our freedom. The wisdom of the causeway reveals the opposite. To reach the ground of our being is the only true security there is, but it will usually feel like the loss of what we had trusted to hold us safe. To become 'grounded' on the bedrock of our being turns out to be the only trustworthy pathway to real freedom.

Of course, we are human, and we need our bridges. Certainly the child needs the womb, and needs to leave the womb. He needs his mother's breast, and he needs to be weaned from his mother's breast. She needs to go to school, and she needs to leave school. There are bridges that we need, and bridges that we must eventually let go of, to trust the bedrock that is revealed only by the causeway. And there is the ultimate loss, in the burial place, which may prove to be the ultimate gateway to life.

A cosmic flush and a rainbow bridge

All our lives, from time to time, come up against an apparently intractable obstruction. We stand face to face with a 'No Through Road' sign. Many of the crisis points in our experience are places like this. Either there seems to be no way forward at all, or all the ways that are open to us appear to be equally impassable or unacceptable.

When the place of transition feels like this, a bridge can give us its own special kind of encouragement. It can help us to refuse to be stopped in our tracks. Whatever else a bridge may be, it is always a symbol of the refusal to take 'No' for an answer. It comes to the brink of the uncrossable – and then crosses it! It can give us a deep assurance that there is always a way, though we may have to search hard to find it, or even build it ourselves. And we may have to go against common sense to do so! Many of the changes and advances in human life and understanding, and all new thrusts of evolution, have grown out of difficulties that had to be overcome, and from pioneering people who were willing to risk the bridges of transition with no certainties about what was waiting on the other side.

Such a situation faced an old man and his family in an ancient legend that pervades the collective storytelling of many different peoples and cultures. We may be most familiar with this man under the name of Noah.

At the first station on our Celtic Way, we encountered the story of how human hearts first turned into 'islands' and lost their connectedness to the bedrock oneness of creation. Once this process of disintegration into island-individualism had begun, there was no way of preventing the consequences. Individuals were pitched into competition with each other. The first stirrings of jealousy muddied the waters of friendship and love. Jealousy led to violence and the entire fabric of God's Dream started to unravel and to become tangled into terrible knots, strangling human hearts and hopes.

We know this pattern of disintegration in our own experience. We know its destructive outcome. When it begins to happen in our lives, we might feel that we want to flush the whole thing away and start again, with a clean slate and a fresh chance. The story of Noah is perhaps one of the ways in which the whole human race expresses this desire to flush away the mess and start over again. It also tells us something of the truth expressed in the Scottish proverb: *Man's extremity is God's opportunity*.

Here is an imaginative retelling of Noah's story as it appears in the book of Genesis (chapters 6 to 8). As you read it, let it speak to you of anything in your own life that feels so impossible to resolve that you wish you could flush it away, and then notice how the story envisages God dealing with such feelings:

God looked down on the Earth and wept to see the unravelling of his eternal Dream. Each creature seemed to be pulling, relentlessly, on its own little strand, and no one could see that the integrity of the whole of creation was being torn apart. Their eyes had dimmed so much, and their focus had shortened so dramatically, that they were blinded to what they were doing to each other. It felt like the end of the road. An awakening from a dream that had turned into a nightmare.

God's tears fell upon creation. They gathered into a running stream, and grew into a raging river. It was a river that could not be crossed. It became a flood that covered the Earth. No repair work would mend this broken Dream. To all God's pleadings for a return to wholeness and sanity, the answer came re-echoing back from every corner of creation: 'No!'

And it was then that God refused to take 'No!' for an answer. Surely, he pondered, life is stronger than death, and creation is stronger than destruction. And, contrary to all human common sense and reason, God resolved to build a bridge across the waters of destruction. It would be a bridge to new possibilities and new beginnings, but it would demand of humankind a special kind of trust and courage. It would be a bridge that called upon men and women to work as co-creators in their own future. This challenge would call them beyond their present limits, but it was the only way to move beyond the impasse.

God moved unseen among the sons and daughters of Earth, and came across Noah. Noah was a man who had lived a long, long life and had struggled to keep the fire of God's Dream burning in his own heart and in the hearts of his children. God decided to take a chance on Noah's trust and courage, and his ability to dream big, unreasonable dreams. He asked him to build a boat.

'Noah,' God said, 'soon my grief will wash the world away, but you shall build an ark to carry you and your children and grandchildren safely across the flood waters. Will you trust me for a new beginning out of all this destruction? Together we can begin again, in new ways, to dream my Dream again for a new generation. If you will trust me, then build an ark as I shall instruct you, and when the ark is ready, take on board your own family, and take a male and female of every species of living creature. You and they shall be the seedcorns of a new beginning.'

And Noah trusted the Dream and built his ark. And when

*it was ready he and his family went on board, taking with them a
male and female of every kind of creature. Thus the seed of the
future was cast upon the waters that had flushed the past away.*

*Noah was the last to board the ark, and as he did so, God
closed the door behind him. Once the future had been entrusted to
this fragile bridge, there was no way back.*

*For forty days the ark, with its cargo of hope and promise,
tossed on the seas of despair. The waters that appeared to be
destroying all life, all hope, were the same waters that floated
the little ark of promise and set it free to search out the new
beginnings. Eventually a fresh wind blew over the face of the
Earth, and ever so gradually the waters began to ebb.*

*Noah tentatively opened a porthole and peered outside. Still
there was nothing in sight except water. He sent out a dove, but
after a while the dove returned, because she could find nowhere to*

perch, out in the watery world. Noah waited for seven more days, and sent the dove out again. In the evening the dove returned, but this time she was carrying a sprig from an olive tree in her beak. Noah realized then that dry land was emerging out of the devastation. He waited a further seven days and sent the dove out for a third time. And she never returned. And so it was that Noah knew the dry land had returned. The ark came to rest on the higher slopes of a mountain. Noah opened the hatches, and set free the seed of the new beginning.

God rejoiced to see his Dream reborn. He desired to mark this moment eternally, as a sign to all creation that hope is more real and permanent than despair. He shone his perfect, invisible light – the light of joy – through all the tears that would ever flow out of human grief and suffering. That invisible light was broken down, through our tears, into all the colours of the rainbow. And

*God stretched the rainbow across the heavens, so that we might
never forget the promise that holds all creation in being. This is the
promise that life and joy are the permanent reality, like the blue of
the sky, and that all the roadblocks we encounter are like the clouds
– black and threatening perhaps, but never the final word. Because
the final word is always 'Yes!'*

We can re-enact the story of Noah many times over in our
lives. Some of us may be more prone than others to fall into the
black pits of despair when we come up against some major
obstruction or dislocation in our lives. However, few of us will
escape situations when we have to decide whether to succumb
to despair, or to search for, or build, a bridge to take us over the
obstacle and open up new possibilities. It is the choice between
taking 'No!' for an answer, or asserting our 'Yes!' to life.

The story of Noah gives us some wisdom along the way:

● We may have to trust our intuition, rather than our common
sense, when it comes to searching for, or building, a bridge
over the troubled waters;

● We will need to stay true to our first instinct that it is better to
travel hopefully towards life than to surrender to the destructive
forces within or around us;

● We carry within ourselves – within the 'ark' of our own
experience – the seeds of every new beginning. They dwell
in the sacred, and indestructible, core of our being;

● It may take a long time to navigate the devastation of the
situation in which we find ourselves, but solid ground will
return if we wait expectantly, and observantly;

● The setting out upon the new beginning may need to be done
in stages, testing the ground as we go.

And bridges, of course, are fragile affairs. They are the first
target of enemy action, because to destroy them is a way of

bringing the whole system to its knees and undermining the communication throughout our bedrock wholeness. No surprise, then, that our attempts at hope are so often and so easily undermined by the pressures of pessimism and cynicism. Paradoxically, too, experience reveals that the most fragile bridges are often the most secure. We can fold up our rope bridges and carry them with us, to help us over the next obstacle, while the grand constructions, like our false floors, are not necessarily as safe as they seem. God's rainbow bridge was made of 'thin air', yet it symbolizes a portable promise that can be carried lightly by a pilgrim people.

Crossing the anxiety threshold

It may not be a block or obstruction that plunges us into a place of transition, however. Sometimes our times of change and crisis feel more like being squeezed through a small space and driven forward along a narrow pathway out into the unknown, with the sea swirling either side of us, and the tide sweeping in behind us, cutting off any possibility of retreat.

The causeway is one of the most haunting symbols of this kind of crisis experience. A causeway does just what its name suggests. It causes a way to open up. It is a natural crossing point, often from the mainland out to a tidal island, or between two islands or outcrops of rock. It is only accessible at low tide, when the dry land and solid ground of the causeway are exposed.

The movement of the tide over a causeway can generate a magical fascination. I discovered this to be true one summer afternoon on the north-east coast of England, when I turned down the small road that leads to the shore and the start of the causeway from the mainland to the tidal island of Lindisfarne. To my surprise I found a large number of people gathered there: small babies, toddlers, teenagers, parents and grandparents. Every age group was represented. But they were not waiting to cross the causeway. They were simply standing there watching the tide come in, and some of them remained there for an hour or more. There was a hush of reflective peace over the scene. It was obvious these people knew very well that they were standing on sacred ground. Their quiet, communal gazing upon the incoming water felt like prayer.

Our inner 'causeways' are not always so peaceful. In fact they often seem to arise out of chaos rather than calm. When I think of some of my own life's experiences that have felt like crossing a causeway, I realize they have usually arisen out of a sense of urgency, or drivenness, or unwelcome change. Indeed, causeways only appear when the tide drains away from the bedrock and leaves it exposed – or, possibly, when the harsh winter weather causes land that was hitherto an impassable swamp to freeze over and permit access. In the same way, it is often the experiences of being 'drained' and 'exposed', or 'frozen with fear', that open up these unexpected thresholds of growth and change in our lives. And it is because they are indeed thresholds of *growth* that they become sacred space. They enable us to pass from 'this world' of what we know, to the 'other world' of what is still unknown and untried. The place where we make such crossings is where we do our growing.

My own earliest memory of the 'causeway' feeling was of an incident that happened when I was a small child. My mother had taken me to a nearby playground. At first I was thrilled at embarking on this new adventure, and eager to try out all that was on offer. In particular I gravitated towards what, to me, seemed like a mountainously high slide. I joined the queue to climb the ladder. I set my feet on the first rungs. I began to climb. The higher I got, the more I panicked. Behind me were a dozen or more children, climbing the ladder after me. They were like that incoming tide, cutting off my retreat, and pushing me on and on, to the top of this fearful ladder. I looked down at my mother, still standing on solid ground, and I realized she couldn't guess how frightened I was of what was going to happen when I reached the top of the slide and had to make my downward plunge.

Eventually I reached the top, having almost made up my

mind that I was going to turn back and climb down past all the children waiting behind me. But of course my pride wouldn't let me. If the 'causeway' hadn't closed in behind me that day, I might never have conquered my fear of big slides in big playgrounds. As it was, I slid down with my eyes tightly closed and my heart thumping. And somewhere, deep down, I must have enjoyed it, because I went back to join the queue waiting at the bottom of the ladder again.

Would that all our crisis points were as easily overcome as my encounter with the slide! We will all have our own memories of 'causeway crossings'. Perhaps the feeling of being away from home for the first time and being on the point of dropping out of the new life as a student, or the new job, and rushing home to safe ground again. Perhaps stepping out of a destructive relationship and facing the world on our own for the first time, maybe feeling that anything at all would have been more bearable than this lonely uncertainty. Crossing the causeways of our lives can feel like being squeezed through the eye of a needle. Our life seems to have slipped out of our control and our reactions can no longer be predicted. Perhaps, subconsciously, these times recall our very first causeway crossing, when we were squeezed out of the safety of our mother's womb and into the trauma of birth.

Peter, a friend of Jesus of Nazareth, did some remarkable growing one stormy night out on the local lake, as we learn from Matthew's Gospel, chapter 14. The waters of Galilee were subject to sudden, unpredictable squalls. A group of Jesus' friends was making the lake crossing alone, in the early hours of the morning, before dawn. They had had an amazing day. Jesus had attracted huge crowds, who had followed them up to the hills and showed no sign of wanting to go home, even when evening came. As the friends crossed the waters in their little fishing boat, they were still debating what exactly had happened. One minute they had been working out a way to get food for everyone, out there in the middle of nowhere. Then a child's packed lunch of bread and fish had been handed over to Jesus and the next thing anyone knew he was getting them to take whole baskets of food round to the crowds. Probably they would never know how the thousands of people got fed that night. Meanwhile they were becoming increasingly aware that a nasty storm was brewing. They turned their attention to the boat, and the deteriorating weather conditions:

'It's too bad he sent us off into this weather on our own,' one of them complained, 'when the wind is against us.'

'He's gone into the hills to pray,' another interrupted. 'I guess his prayer is more powerful than anything we can do out here in this wind. Let's trust it.'

They struggled on, as the wind speed increased relentlessly and the boat was pitched like a cork among the thrashing waves. It was then that they noticed a shadowy figure coming towards them through the spray. In the dark, and in their fear, they thought they were seeing a ghost. What else would be coming so close here in the middle of the lake, if not some apparition conjured up by their overwearied minds. But they all saw it, whatever it was. That much was sure.

They fell silent, in terror, cowering in the depths of the boat. Until a familiar voice reached them through the howling of the wind. 'Don't be afraid. It's me.'

Peter was the first to find his voice: 'Lord, is this real? If this is really you, and not some fearful fantasy, call me to come to you across the water.'

The others were aghast. What did Peter think he was saying? Had he completely taken leave of his senses? And then the calm, penetrating voice replied, 'Come!'

Everyone held their breath. What would Peter do now, they asked themselves, but no one dared to speak. Peter himself began to shake. They watched as his face grew tense and the knuckles of his clenched hands whitened. He stepped back, shocked, from the edge of the boat. For a moment he clutched his head with both hands, as if gulping for courage from his closed palms. Then, with a single, determined leap, he vaulted over the side of the boat.

For just a few moments time stood still that night, there in the vortex of the storm. Creation itself seemed to freeze into an expectant stillness as Peter made those first steps of pure faith across the water to his Lord. His entire being was focused on the figure out there in front of him, standing on the water. His whole life energy was pouring into this one single act of total trust, and his eyes were fixed on his friend, standing with outstretched arms, waiting to receive him.

Then for a split second that steady gaze was distracted by the sight of an approaching wave. Peter lost his focus. Fear took over again where trust had reigned. He began to sink. He called out in his panic, and immediately those outstretched arms were round his waist, drawing him gently back on board the boat. 'It was the fear that let you down,' Jesus explained to him, without reproach. 'Let the fear go, and you will discover a whole new layer of trust underneath, and things will become possible that you could never have imagined.'

Peter lay, trembling, in the bottom of the boat. But he had learned the measure of himself that night. And he had recognized the true stature of his friend.

Peter passed, one might say, through the eye of a needle that night. He entered into the heart of his own fear, and was almost destroyed by it. Yet it was precisely in the passage through the heart of the fear that he discovered a new degree of courage, which in turn precipitated a new surge of spiritual growth within him. He passed across a causeway, and was not destroyed.

Mathematicians and scientists, at the start of this third millennium, are exploring 'chaos theory', and discovering that the natural world reveals a mysterious, pervasive pattern of regeneration and growth out of what appears to be a point of near destruction. Perhaps, too, our causeway experiences can truly be called 'chaos causeways'. We sense when we are approaching such a point in our lives. We know that we must cross an important threshold, and that this is the only way to evolve to new levels of growth and maturity, but we are deeply afraid, like Peter, to take that step which will take us over the point of no return. It feels like being squeezed down to almost nothing, and trusting that we will emerge on the other side, not only intact, but to some extent transformed by our experience. These times call for great trust, both in ourselves, and in a creation and a creator that, ultimately, mean well with us. They can also be greatly assisted by sharing our journey with a trusted companion – a 'soul-friend' in Celtic language – who will accompany us with affirming love and encouragement across our lives' thresholds.

Nothing can diminish the mystery of our being, because it is infinitely larger than anything we can think or imagine. However, our perpetual longing to reach into the core of that mystery can be frustrated by our equally persistent habit of creating false certainties. Every time we cross a threshold in our lives, we are passing beyond one of these walls of 'certainty' and we are penetrating just a little further into the mystery at the heart of ourselves and of all creation.

Unless the seed dies...

It must have been dark, when a man called Abram engaged in a memorable and history-changing conversation with God (as reported in the book of Genesis, chapter 15). We hear that the night sky was laden with stars, because God led Abram outside and asked him to look up and count them! We can assume he soon gave up the effort, and listened instead to a promise that seemed to be whispered on the night air:

● The fruits of your own life will be as abundant as the stars. You will be the father of many nations;

- The land around you shall be yours for ever. Though your people shall know exile, they shall never be excluded from their homeland;

- The covenant of oneness between God and his creation shall never be broken;

Abram must often have wondered about these promises, as his life progressed:

- His wife appeared to be barren, and for a long time (until their only son Isaac arrived) there was no sign of even one child, let alone 'many nations' of them;

- The only land Abram was ever to possess was a little field that he bought, as a burial place for his wife Sarah;

- History was to unfold a whole catalogue of disaster, exile and destruction that would cause many to doubt whether they were in the hands of a benevolent God.

Yet today millions of people on planet Earth regard Abram, who became known as Abraham, as the father of their faith. And through their faith journeying they have come to know a deeper truth about the meaning of a spiritual homeland and the bedrock benevolence of the creation that gives them birth and the energizing spirit that gives life to that creation.

The waiting time
Abraham had to wait for the fulfilment of the promise. Perhaps he is still waiting, waiting in faith, yet observing minute by minute the growth of the buried seed of that covenant promise.

He has to wait in the same way that we have to wait for the tide to be right before we can cross the causeway, or for a fertilized egg to become a living child.

The Greeks knew there are two kinds of time and they had different words for them. *Chronos*, on one hand, expressed their notion of time as a way of measuring, in a linear way, the movement of the minutes, the hours, the years and the millennia. *Kairos*, on the other hand, expressed their sense that there is a right and significant moment for action or change. Shakespeare expresses the same intuition in the words of Brutus:

> *There is a tide in the affairs of men,*
> *Which, taken at the flood, leads on to fortune;*
> *Omitted, all the voyage of their life*
> *Is bound in shallows and in miseries.*
> *On such a full sea are we now afloat;*
> *And we must take the current when it serves,*
> *Or lose our venture.*
>
> JULIUS CAESAR ACT 4, SCENE 3

For us, *chronos* is, perhaps, the waiting time, and *kairos* is the moment to respond. *Kairos* is often the catalyst for transformation. It is the moment when we take the risk, build the bridge, cross the causeway, trusting in our instinct to move forward, even though our common sense may tempt us to hold back.

We spend our '*chronos* time', as it were, in a waiting room. Our first waiting room is our mother's womb, our last is the grave. Both are crossing places, from one form of being to another. It may often appear to us, with our limited consciousness, that nothing is happening and none of the promises of life are being fulfilled. So, too, would it appear to a bulb, buried in the cold earth in autumn, and waiting through the long winter months for the promise of its flowering to be fulfilled. Unless the seed 'dies', and surrenders to the long wait of the '*chronos* time', it will never experience the explosion of new birth in the '*kairos* moment'.

Paradoxically, God's promise to Abraham appeared to be fulfilled in a meagre burial plot, where he buried Sarah, the love of his life. Perhaps our deepest dreams may be lying buried in the very place where we have buried our hopes and laid to rest our lives' disappointments. What we leave behind, however, is never lost, but has already been incorporated into who we are, to become a vital component in all we shall become.

You might like to reflect on some of the 'waiting times' in your own experience, and how they have yielded to new growth at the right moment. Visit, in your imagination, the 'burial plots' of your experience, the places where you have buried your disappointed dreams. Grieve there, as you must, but let your tears water the soil and become not the last word on loss, but the first word calling new life into being. At these 'burial plots' you are standing between two worlds – between the old, the known and understood, and the new beginning which still lies beyond the scope of your wildest imagining. You are standing in sacred space, because it is on the very edge of the known that the infinite possibilities of the unknown begin to unfold.

Seasons of commissioning

Every season of our lives will lead us to its own threshold experiences and crossing places. At such transition points we move on, often painfully, to the next stage of our personal growth, leaving behind the known and trusted, in order to receive, with empty, open hands, the new and unfamiliar. Behind us on such causeways, the tide rolls in, cutting off our retreat, and we know, if we dare to admit it to ourselves, that nothing will ever be the same again.

As we stand on such thresholds, life itself is commissioning us to move onto a new stage of our 'Becoming'. Something at the core of our being is urging us forward into the next phase of our personal evolution, as surely as the onset of labour pain and the breaking of the waters commission the expectant mother to begin the process of birthing.

The pain at such points can be very real, yet it is always

the pain of growth, not of destruction. Indeed, it is a fact of nature that the seasons of growth and change are also the seasons of maximum vulnerability. The burgeoning of springtime always coincides with the months when the winds are high and the lingering late frosts threaten the survival of the new buds. The glory of autumn walks hand in hand with the October gales and the November fogs. So, too, our most obvious human seasons of change – in adolescence and in mid-life – are fraught with vulnerability, with inner questioning and with disturbing physical and emotional upheaval.

These seasons signal a change of direction in our lives. They are 'chaos causeways'. We have no choice but to venture across them, but they are charged with promise. They are sacred space, with the power to transform us.

Celebrating our transitions

We can, however, assist at the birth of each new stage of growth, by offering each other encouragement and companionship through these crucial eye-of-the-needle passages. We can *commission* each other for the way ahead. In the rituals of organized religion, this kind of commissioning may take the form of the sacrament of ordination for a particular ministry. In daily life our 'commissionings' may take many forms:

- A person starting out on a new job, for example, may be welcomed by his future colleagues and initiated in some celebratory way into the new culture. He may also be put through an induction course to train him for his new responsibilities.

- A student leaving home to begin studies at college may experience a kind of commissioning in Freshers' Week, with all that that entails! And at the other end of her course of studies, a graduation ceremony in the presence of her family and peers will commission her to go forward into a new stage of life where she will put into practice what she has been studying.

- Retirement, redundancy, or simply a decision to leave paid employment to do other things that seem more important, are passages into a new and often uncertain future. They can be marked by a leaving party, at which former colleagues launch us into a new way of life.

- When personal loss has to be lived through, and bereavement faced, the presence of friends and family at a memorial gathering is a way of commissioning the bereaved person to walk on in courage, and with their support, into the new and challenging days ahead.

Our generation has experienced one of the most significant collective crossing places of all. We have crossed the threshold of a new millennium. Individually we may have celebrated this significant moment in all kinds of ways. But collectively, as a friend commented to me at the time, the entire world, for the very first time, shared in each others' celebrations by means of global television. Thus we witnessed a tide of darkness and light sweeping across the Earth from East to West, and we participated in every nation's greeting of the midnight hour and their welcoming of the first dawn of the new age. The light of life itself appeared to be passing from people to people like an Olympic torch, and as it did so the longing for peace and love was re-echoed, not shallowly but from the heart, around the globe. Each time zone commissioned the next to carry forward the hope of us all.

When we cross our personal crisis thresholds, or chaos causeways, we may feel very far from celebratory, but at that moment – that *sacred* moment – we, too, are carrying a torch of life forward into new possibilities. We are stepping over the known boundaries. And boundaries, as we shall see at the next and final stopping place on our pilgrimage, are at the heart of the whole Celtic intuition of sacred space.

bOUNDARIES

BORDERLANDS OF BEING

One October afternoon I was working at my desk, bathed in a pool of mellow light streaming in through the window. Outside the window was an oak tree, splendid in its autumn glory. The tree was pure magic, and the afternoon light was loaded with a deep, heavy presence, shot through with gold, and with the power to make that oak tree look like the very first oak tree in the first Dream of creation.

Then I heard a tapping sound somewhere else in the house, becoming ever more insistent. I searched all around, but failed to find any obvious cause, until I happened to look out of a window on the opposite side of the house. To my amazement I could see it was pouring with rain there, and the noise I could hear was the pounding of the rain on the rooftop. Back in the study, however, the sun still shone down, setting the autumn

leaves alight in the oak tree. One half of the house was in a rainstorm; the other half was bathed in powerful autumn light. I was standing exactly on the boundary between rain and shine. It felt strangely holy, and the oak tree took on the mystery of a burning bush, bathed in fire, yet not consumed.

There is something profoundly mysterious about boundaries. On a boundary, like the one I have described, we stand, as it were, looking in two directions at once. We can see both ways, and those different views may be very different indeed – even irreconcilable – within the limits of our human thinking and imagining. Such a place may seem to be rather remote from normal experience. After all, it isn't every day that we find ourselves on the border of two weather systems. Yet we do find ourselves, twice a day, on the boundary of light and darkness, and for most people there is a deep fascination with these times of dawn and dusk, when the Earth seems to hold its breath. In Celtic language, these are moments experienced 'between two worlds', and they feel holy, in ways we find hard to express. Similar feelings may arise as we walk along a seashore, and experience the magnetic attraction of that boundary line between the land and the water, drawn afresh with every new wave that breaks.

All the stations along our Celtic pilgrimage have been about boundary space of one kind or another. This is because the very essence of sacred space lies in its location at a point where the visible and the invisible meet and interpenetrate, opening up new energy and insight. At this, our final station, we reach the edge of the mystery, and reflect on what it might mean to see beyond the borderlands of our being.

Boundaries – little and large

Boundaries can be daunting. At our last station, the crossing places of our lives revealed their potential for pitching us into chaos, as well as their promise to lead us to new stages of growth. But there are personal boundary spaces we can explore safely within the limits of our own minds and bodies and in the familiar places of home and the natural world in which we live. They remind us of the sacredness of the space in which our everyday lives are lived.

Our Earth, as we have already noticed, takes us to boundary land every day of the year. The moments of sunrise and sunset, for most people, have a special kind of power. Which of us has never stopped, spellbound, to watch the sun rise above the horizon, or sink into the sea or behind the hills, at dusk. To be out and about at sunrise or sunset feels like 'walking the edges of the day', when there seems to be a holy stillness across the Earth. Then the day begins, or the night, and we are back in our 'reality', but left with the feeling that we have experienced something of a greater, perhaps eternal, reality. The desire to touch the mystery of our being at these points where it feels especially close seems to be universal.

Our own bodies also take us to boundary ground, where 'the veil is thin':

- The delicate membrane of our skin, with its myriad nerve endings, is so easily damaged, yet also so sensitive to the world around us. Our skin is our 'boundary space', where 'we' come into direct contact with all that is 'other'. In very practical ways, this is where change and growth and transformation are kindled. We receive the signals of the world beyond us, through our senses, and we react to what we receive. We are changed by it, however slightly. Perhaps we grow a little in understanding and appreciation of what is 'not us', or perhaps we change direction in response to a warning signal. If such boundary interchange were to fail, we would die.

- Our eyes are another 'hole in the veil'. We may manage to keep ourselves safely aloof from those around us, but this defence breaks down when there is eye-to-eye contact. Our eyes are deeply vulnerable, yet they are the place where we cannot hide our truth. Our eyes reveal our souls, to those who have eyes to see. They also shed our tears and light up with our smiles. They are the windows upon our true self, and another boundary space where we meet others in an intimacy we cannot disguise.

● An embryonic sac held us all in being while we were preparing for birth. Then the moment came for the breaching of that membrane. The waters broke, and we were on our way towards the huge and unknown 'otherness' of the world beyond ourselves. The little tear in the embryonic membrane became, in a very real way, the 'hole in the veil' and the gateway to the fullness of human life. This encourages me to believe that the natural life I lead is also held within a veil I cannot penetrate by my own efforts, but which sometimes becomes thin and translucent, to reveal moments of promise of something so much greater, still beyond my consciousness.

Our homes, too, contain clues about the 'veil'. I have noticed that whenever I go into a room where I haven't been before, I gravitate immediately towards the window. I find myself fascinated, at some deep, subconscious level, by the view beyond the window. The room has its own powerful reality, and gives me a space to be, but the view draws my vision towards something beyond, and the window is the 'hole in the veil'. The window is the gateway between my present place of being and the place beyond. It is borderland, allowing me to be present simultaneously, to both the 'here' and the 'not here'.

Our early ancestors knew how to celebrate sacred space on a grand scale. A visit to Stonehenge, for example, reveals that the stones are arranged to catch precisely the point of sunset and sunrise for the winter and summer solstices respectively. To experience these moments of sunrise and sunset, with the sun's rays piercing the gap in the stones and flooding the inner circle, is to be taken out of time. It is impossible not to feel very close to these 'primitive' peoples in their sense of awe and wonder – a sense so strong that it gave them the energy to drag massive boulders for hundreds of miles across the countryside.

Can we have any doubt that these ancestors of ours had a sense of what we might call 'the transcendent', that we still possess, but mainly keep locked up in the closets of our private lives. They were quite deliberately 'making a hole' in the veil that divides the natural world from all that is beyond it. And they were celebrating the inpouring of 'otherness' into their everyday lives.

Piercing the veil

The poet Gerard Manley Hopkins reminds us, 'The world is charged with the grandeur of God.' It shimmers like 'shook foil', and something deep within us longs to be in touch with the vast 'otherness' and to find ways of expressing it. Unconsciously, perhaps, we are always looking for ways of being on the boundaries of mystery. And we don't need to drag huge boulders across the countryside. Let us look instead at some of the things we are actually engaged in. You might like to reflect on some of these suggestions:

- Have you spent time gazing at the night sky, or walking the shoreline?

- Have you taken a walk at sunrise or sunset recently?

- Have you grappled with the story of the universe and its beginnings, and pondered the big questions of where we came from and where we are going? Have you looked at the night sky through a telescope? Or have you looked through a microscope, at the universe revealed in a single cell?

- Have you known moments in a personal relationship, when the boundaries between you and an intimate friend seemed to dissolve, in an awareness of deep, unspoken love and understanding?

- Have you stopped to speak to someone who is on the margins of society? Perhaps you have shared a sandwich, or a friendly smile with them.

- Have you taken time out to visit someone in hospital or in prison, or to write a letter to someone who appears to have fallen 'over the edge' of what we call respectability?

- Can you remember any dreams you have had, that seemed to speak to your heart from somewhere far beyond, perhaps leaving you with new insight about the way forward in some issue?

- Have you ever attended a birth, or accompanied someone up to the threshold of death? Have you held a newborn child in your arms, or cradled the head of a dying loved one?

- Have you ever been part of a conversation in which two or more people from different disciplines or walks of life have suddenly become aware of a whole new way of looking at a problem, when they stepped over the boundaries of their usual thinking patterns?

- Have you written a poem, drawn a picture, sung a song, joined in a dance, skied down a mountainside, spent time in quiet meditation? Have you felt the breath of the divine rushing through your lungs as you did any of these, or any other things that have transported you beyond the fences of your own island world?

These are all examples of human activities that touch the boundaries of experience. If any of these suggestions has struck a chord with you, have you shared your feelings with anyone else? If not, do you feel able to do so now, simply by telling a trusted friend about your moment 'on the boundary' and how you felt about it, and then listening as they share their experience with you?

Archways to eternity

As we have seen, all crossing places, such as bridges, causeways and burial grounds, are sacred space in the Celtic vision, because they lead us onto the boundary ground and beyond it. But what happens, we must ask, when the gateways are blocked?

- When the clouds of depression are low and there is no sense of sunrise;
- When the eyes are sightless;
- When the womb is unfruitful or the child stillborn;
- When the room has no windows but only prison bars.

It is my joy to know personally one or two people whose gates are barred in these ways. I have a friend who is blind, a friend who is imprisoned in a foreign country, a friend who is painfully childless and a friend who is clinically depressed.

These are people who, we could say, stand on the edge of the edges. They are those who already have one foot over the boundary. My friendship with these people is a special blessing, because they have shown me, in their lives, what it means to be forced, by circumstance, beyond the signposts to the destination. For me they are like the arch that supports the open gateway to eternity, and carries the weight of our freedom to pass back and forth across its boundary. Or they are like the stones of the bridge that leads through the gap in the veil, but must bear the weight of our tramping feet. Along with all those whom society drives to the edges, all the 'marginalized', these people are icons of holiness to me, their lives stretched out in pain in order to hold open the doorways to eternity, so that all might see beyond, and glimpse the 'place of resurrection'.

A man of mystery

In chapter 3 we met Moses, and shared in his encounter with the burning bush that was to give him new energy for a new mission. That mission was, ultimately, to bring him up against a boundary he could not cross – the edge of a mystery he could not penetrate.

From the very beginning Moses was a man of mystery. Under threat of death, as we recall, he had been committed by his mother to a basket and left to drift on the river, concealed among the reeds, there to be discovered by Pharaoh's daughter.

His ending is likewise swathed in mystery. He died on the mountainside overlooking the Promised Land, but his body was never found. His life spans the early history of his human community, like a rainbow, beginning and ending in the unknown, yet charged with the kind of radiance that makes a difference to all those it falls upon.

Moses was a man who talked with God. He also had the wisdom to know that God, however we understand the word, is a dynamic power. He met his God in a tent, the Tent of Meeting, and encouraged his people to do the same. Let us join them now as they set out on their journey through the desert to the Promised Land. This part of their story is told in the book of Exodus (chapters 33 and 34). We are all engaged in a journey like this. Some of us might name it 'the spiritual journey' or 'the journey of the heart', leading us from where we are today, into all the experience and growth that will make us into who we have the potential to become. For others this journey may have a wider meaning. We may see it as the story of the evolution, physical and spiritual, of all creation, from that first microscopic atom from which creation, as we currently understand it, erupted and expanded into a living, teeming universe. Let us simply take whatever picture we personally have of this mysterious 'journey', and walk for a while alongside these early wanderers, seeking their tomorrow out of the ashes of their yesterday:

God said to Moses, 'Move on from here. Make the people move on. The journey is a moving, living journey, and you can never establish it anywhere in one fixed place. As you journey, you will catch glimpses of my radiance flashing through your lives. Notice them. Engage with them – with your hearts, and not just with your heads. That's where you will draw your energy for the way.'

Moses took this advice to heart. He took a tent with him on the trek, calling it the Tent of Meeting. It was to be the space where he, and his people, might go deep into their hearts and engage with those charges of God's radiance that would come. He pitched the tent always outside the place where they were camping, because it was a special space. It was a space, not a place. It was a space beyond their normal understanding of place, and it was a gateway to moments of eternity beyond their normal understanding of time.

Today for us, as for our ancestors, the tent-space takes many forms. Sometimes it is a space for individual prayer or meditation, a quiet corner with a candle. Sometimes it is more like a gathering place for all, in a communal searching for the mystery. Sometimes it is a flash of awareness that we and all creation are one, eternally interwoven. Sometimes it is a pleading space, where tears are poured out and grief expressed. It takes many shapes, perhaps, but always it is a moving space, carried forward day by day.

Moses felt at home in the Tent. He went there regularly and when he came out his face would be shining, as if he had absorbed something of the eternal radiance. Yet even for Moses there was a boundary line. He begged God to reveal his face. 'Please show me the fullness of your glory,' he pleaded. 'I have stood so often on the brink of your unimaginable Being, and I long to know it completely.' God was moved by Moses' pleading, but he knew that no human being could survive an encounter with the source of all Being.

'I am the source of creation,' said God, 'and I am the essence of Life itself. You cannot look into my face and live. But walk in my presence and your own lives shall be creative and full. You will draw freely on my living energy in all you do that springs from the well of truth deep in your hearts. Your lives will become a journey rich in promise, towards a destination that is like a land fertile with streams and plentiful harvests, where your physical hunger and your inner aching shall all be satisfied. Journey in my presence and in my strength and all this shall be the 'place of resurrection' for all creation. But if you try to journey in your own strength, you will fall and wither along the way. I am the source of Life. Choose Life, in every moment of your living, because this is the whole purpose of your existence.'

It was a long journey for Moses and his people, as it is for all who venture into the journey of Life, but at last they came close to their destination. Moses climbed to the peak of Pisgah, just opposite

Jericho. From there he could see the whole countryside spread out before him, and there, for the final time in his mortal life, he heard the voice of God: 'This is the land I promised to your ancestors and to your descendants,' God told him. 'You have led them faithfully to its boundaries, and I have shown you this vision of the destination of all your journeying. But in this life you cannot enter into it. This is a boundary you cannot cross. Creation itself is not yet ready for its final place of resurrection, yet you have been a gateway to future generations, who will pass beyond this place, trusting always in the promise of Life itself drawing them beyond the certainties of today into the mysteries of tomorrow.'

And there Moses died, crossing the ultimate boundary of his own life on Earth. The people believed God himself had buried Moses, up there on the mountain, because to this day no one has ever discovered his grave.

Just before he died, Moses did one last thing. He blessed his people, tribe by tribe, and anointed them for the onward journey. Although he himself passed into mystery, his spirit moved on in those he had blessed.

Border country – friend or foe?

But there are other boundaries than these, and some of them impact our lives considerably. Our whole world and most of our institutions are divided by boundaries, many of which have a hostile, or, at the very least, a defensive intention. At such places the feeling is, generally, not one of holiness, and wholeness, but of division and exclusion.

What makes the difference, we might ask, between a hostile boundary and a boundary that marks the edges of new growth? One aspect of the difference seems to lie in the question: 'Is this boundary forcing me to make a choice between two or more mutually exclusive possibilities (an '*either/or*' situation), or is it inviting me to move to a new stage of growth that includes *both* the place I am coming from *and* the place I am moving into?'

Most of our national and political boundaries, for example, are *either/or* lines, creating exclusion zones. The boundary on which Moses stood to view the Promised Land was a *both–and* boundary, allowing him to stand on the known side of the mystery and yet be in touch with the vision of all that was still to come.

Another important difference between the two kinds of boundary seems to be that *protective* boundaries are created out of *fear*, while the sacred, *prophetic* boundaries of new growth mark the edges of our deep human *desire* to grow in love and understanding and awareness.

And so we have a real and a pressing choice as to how we react to the boundary zones in our lives. We may need to confront and challenge any destructive boundaries that are artificially restricting our freedom to grow and relate with each other more fully. But we also need to remain open to the continual expansion of our innermost being into new realms of awareness and growth.

Pause for a few minutes to reflect on the 'boundary zones' in your own life. Where do you feel restricted? Is the restriction a reasonable one (imposed, for example, for the sake of creating safe and harmonious living conditions within your family or workplace), or is it artificially restrictive (forcing you to keep a set of rules and 'toe the party line' within a group or institution you belong to, for example)? If you feel uneasy about what you find, is there anything you would like to do to change things? Which boundaries in your life would you choose to accept and comply with? Which would you want to confront and challenge?

Now take a look at your own 'circles'. Who is 'in' and who is 'out' of them? Are you happy with these arrangements? Is there anything you would wish to change? Which of the boundaries in your personal life do you feel are inward-looking and based on fear and the need to exclude what feels threatening? Which are outward-looking and express a desire to grow and move forward? In what areas of your life can you see yourself as a border guard, trying to keep out thoughts, ideas or experiences you are not ready to face? In which areas do you feel rather that you are 'pushing the boundaries' and responding to a deep urge inside you to move forward, beyond the known of your present experience?

Walking the edges

Let us join a group of friends taking a quiet stroll through the fields of Galilee. It was a Saturday, the Jewish Sabbath, when no work was to be done. A clear demarcation line had been drawn by tradition and religious authority around what might and might not be done on the Sabbath day. It was an exclusion line, stating dogmatically which activities were 'in' and which were 'out' of line.

There are plenty of restrictive boundaries like these in our own lives, and many of them also need to be challenged. As the human spirit evolves to new levels of understanding, we can see how the boundaries of one generation are often called into question by the next, and limitations we once accepted are superseded by new freedoms. The most obvious boundaries of apartheid, for example, which once enforced violent demarcations between people of different races, have been challenged and largely dismantled. The assumption that women have nothing to say and need not be educated has become history in much of the world in the course of just one century. More subtle forms of segregation still remain to be questioned, however, as they make themselves felt in 'members-only' clubs, or elitist cliques within our communities. Unspoken barriers continue to make it clear to minority groups that they are not welcome in particular circles, and misguided social pressures still insist that 'big boys don't cry'. As Eliza Doolittle was to discover, in *My Fair Lady*, even the way we speak can set up a barrier between us and those we would like to be in contact with. The hint of local dialect (to say nothing of the scarf of the local soccer club!) can 'make some other Englishman despise us'.

Such were the rules that put large 'fences' around the field through which these friends were strolling. As they walked, deep in conversation, one of them plucked a few stalks of corn. Perhaps he chewed the grain, or tossed it over the edges of the field. And this brings us to the heart of the matter. He was 'walking the edges' of the field of accepted behaviour. He was pushing the boundaries. It was not permitted to pluck corn on the Sabbath day, yet he did so, with the well-known comment, 'The Sabbath was made for men and women, not men and women for the Sabbath!' He was, it seems, deliberately confronting and challenging a divisive rule. As he cast the grain over the boundary limits, he was not only defying a false exclusion zone, he was sowing the seed of new life beyond the limits of the field in which he found himself. In my inner picture of this incident, new corn is springing up on the other side of the boundary. As a result, the field is growing and spreading, not by conquest, but by the gentle seeding of the one who dares to go beyond the limits.

Breaking bounds or breaking moulds?

When is it creative, and when is it destructive, to 'break bounds'? As a schoolgirl I would often slip away with my friends at lunchtime and quite deliberately climb over the perimeter wall, for no better reason than the sheer pleasure of going 'out of bounds'. In this instance, the rules were intended to protect us from potential dangers beyond the school limits. Our challenge, therefore, was an act of defiance for its own sake. We didn't learn anything on the other side of the wall. There was no growth or new experience, merely a degree of self-satisfaction. Now, as an adult, I try to remember this, when I am tempted to break limits just for the sake of it.

However, there have been other situations when I have been brought up against boundaries that I needed to cross, because they were impeding my inner journey, or that of others. Sometimes these have been boundaries imposed by outside agencies. As a child, for example, in early post-war Britain, I tried to make friends with a German refugee child who arrived in our class. I remember the shock I felt when this friendship was severely discouraged, on the grounds that the boy was deemed to have come from a 'hostile nation'. I can see now that this was a confrontation with a question that wasn't just about the boy and me, but was a challenge to the prejudices of the time. And sometimes the resistance has been from inside myself, when I have been challenged to cross the boundaries of my own 'comfort zone' and do something I thought I couldn't do.

These have all been boundaries inviting me to new growth. They have been calls, not so much to 'break the bounds' as to 'break the moulds'. Moulds keep us fixed in certain ways of thinking and feeling, reacting and doing things, or avoiding doing them. But we are dynamic beings – part of a dynamic universe which is constantly changing and expanding and evolving. Moulds can only hold us secure for so long, and then they have to be broken, if we are to move on, as individuals, and as part of all creation.

A meeting in the garden

In chapter 20 of his gospel, John describes an amazing moment of discovery and growth 'beyond the limits'. It happens on the Sunday following Jesus' crucifixion. Let us join two people in a quiet garden in Jerusalem, as they walk this boundary together:

It had been the longest Sabbath ever. Mary, from the village of Magdala, had been aching to go to the place where her dearest friend had been buried the previous Friday. He had been executed as a dangerous troublemaker. She was still numb from the shock of it all. She knew him better than that. They all did – all his friends. There was nothing she would not do for him, even now. But now was too late. His body had been sealed up in a rock tomb since Friday, and now at last she was free to go and shed her tears at his graveside.

Friday had taken Mary across a terrible boundary in her thinking and feeling. She had been so sure her friend was going to save the world, and that nothing could destroy him. Standing here, at the gateway to this burial garden, brought home to her the undeniable fact that her hopes and dreams had been dashed. She felt as though all she had ever lived for was buried here with him, behind that rock.

The rock! She gasped at what she saw. The rock had moved. And the guards, set there to watch over it, were fast asleep. She peered inside, and all she saw was emptiness. That yawning empty space shook her mind apart, and took her right back to the feelings she had

once had, when her own life had been like a gaping hole, aching with emptiness – until he had come into her life and filled it to the brim.

Hardly aware of what she was doing, Mary ran back into the warm light of the morning sun. In the distance she could see someone tending the plants and raking the path. She went up to him and poured her anxious questions all over him. 'My friend who was buried there – over there,' she cried, 'He's gone! Has someone taken the body away? Please, please tell me where he is if you know!'

The gardener turned round slowly, and laid his rake aside. The light of his eyes seemed to burn into her heart. 'If you've seen someone take him away, please tell me,' she repeated. Then the gardener spoke to her. He spoke her name, and the word was charged, and supercharged, with love:

'Mary!'

'Master?' she whispered, as she ran towards him and flung her arms around him, recognizing the friend she had lost and found again.

'Don't try to hold on to me, Mary,' he said. 'I have crossed the boundary and you cannot fully follow me – not yet. Instead, go back now to our friends, and tell them what you have seen here. Tell them there is nothing to fear. To cross the boundary of death is just a gateway into a new, eternal form of life. You are not yet quite *ready for that birthing. There is still much for you to do here on your side of the boundary. Tell our friends I am going ahead of them to Galilee, and I will be with you in all you still have to do. I will breathe my living energy through all your days. Let me go now, Mary. We cannot return to how things were. We have crossed the threshold now, to how things shall become.'*

Mary crossed her own boundary that morning. She let go of the desire to return to how things had been, and embraced the call to move forward across the threshold into the unknown of how things would become. She returned to the group of friends and became the first apostle of the Christian gospel.

Two kinds of dying led to the boundary where Mary and her friend Jesus met in the garden that first Easter morning. For him it had been a literal, physical dying. For her it was a death of hope and dream. Their story can open up something of the meanings of our own dyings and boundary meetings. Just reflect on whether you identify with any of these:

● Mary had lost the friend who had, truly, transformed her life, and with him, she had lost her trust in the promise of a new world order she had thought he was going to establish there and then. Her own preconceptions had been shattered. There seemed to be nothing to take their place, and she longed for things to return to how they were before Jesus' death.

● She came to the boundary line of life and death through her own aching and grieving, not through any kind of 'achievement'. It is frequently in our sense of loss and emptiness that we come close to the place where the veil is thin – almost never when we are feeling 'satisfied'. The boundaries of being are always places of vulnerability.

● The authorities, afraid that Jesus' death might unleash a riot, had placed guards at the tomb to keep watch. In these sentries we meet exactly the kind of border guards we have recognized as the products of fear and power and wrong authority. They are there to keep contained a power they do not understand. Jesus had 'broken bounds' because his living energy could not be contained by them. Now, mistaken by Mary for the gardener, he draws her gently across the threshold of her fears and encourages her to move forward, one step into the beyond.

- The mystery of all we are seeking may take the form of the everyday, and we may fail to recognize it, precisely because it is so 'normal', just as Mary failed at first to recognize 'the gardener'. If we really desire to reach the meanings beyond the veil, we may need to become much more sensitively aware of the immediacy and the mystery of the created world around us.

- The mystery can break through to us by calling us personally, by our own name. When this happens there can be no more room for doubt. We may doubt doctrine and second-hand wisdom, but we cannot deny what our personal experience reveals. We know the mystery is calling us personally when we feel a tug deep in our innermost being that says, 'This is important. This is for you. Ponder it and listen hard.' Or when we wake from a dream, or leave a time of meditation, knowing that some deep chord inside us has been brought into resonance with Life itself. We all know such feelings, but we find it hard to name them. The important thing is to take them seriously and allow them to begin their transforming action.

- We cannot enclose the mystery. It will always break out of our sealed containers, whether these containers are our own private worlds, or the formulas of doctrinal religion, or the institutions of a carefully ordered society. It will always be bigger than anything we can invent to keep it contained.

- When we recognize the mystery active in our own lives, we must let it go, for it is a dynamic energy, in transit through the fabric and circumstances of our lives. It is a star to follow, not a trophy to possess. It calls us to become mediators of the blessing to the rest of creation, in whatever way our personal desires and vocations suggest.

Boundary seasons

The experience of standing on 'boundary' ground can feel frightening and disturbing. We meet it most obviously when we are faced with the reality of death, either our own or that of someone we love. Perhaps less obviously, we meet it in the many lesser deaths we face as our lives move on, for example, in the death of certainties on which we once based our lives, but can no longer rely on. Such 'deaths' occur when a significant relationship breaks down, a livelihood is lost, or a particular system of belief opens up into a chasm of doubt. The solid ground on which we once stood firm appears to have become a swamp, which will no longer bear our weight. Can such a situation really be 'sacred space'?

In the story of Mary's meeting with the risen Jesus, the boundaries being walked are about all these things – the finality of death, the loss of relationship, the destruction of certainty and the confrontation of doubt.

For the Celtic pilgrim, the ultimate boundary was the letting go of 'place' (or solid ground) and symbolically, or actually, committing oneself to the sea in a small coracle. If we allow ourselves, in imagination, to walk that boundary line between land and sea, and feel the lapping of the tides at our feet, we might gain some sense of what this 'letting go' might mean. On the one side we see the solid ground of what we have lost – the steady job, the cherished relationship, the security of good health, the certainty of received faith. On the other side we see nothing but the expanse of an unpredictable ocean, with no land in sight. Yet this place of boundary, so Celtic wisdom assures us, is sacred.

In Mary's story, too, the ground is hallowed, even though it feels, to her, like a swamp of despair. It is hallowed because it is precisely there that she encounters the call to move to a new stage of growth, and a deeper layer of the 'ground of her being'.

Our boundaries always hold this element of challenge.

Will we try to cling to the solid ground we once knew, but know we have now irretrievably lost? This was Mary's first reaction. Or will we get into that little coracle, and entrust ourselves to the high seas of all that lies beyond, still unknown, untested, unseen? This was Mary's final choice, encouraged by the indestructible presence of her friend, assuring her that creation, ultimately, is benevolent, and that the seas would carry her to new realms of being.

The Pilgrim Fathers set sail in trust across the boundaries of the known world, to discover the New World. We, too, are called across the boundaries of our doubts and fears, to discover new possibilities which will only open up to us when we have let go of certainties that are too small for us. Faith, at this point, ceases to be a statement of belief in a set of facts. It becomes a call to transcend the limits of today and journey on towards Forever.

Samuel's new coat

There is a lovely story in the first book of Samuel about a mother who chose to let go of what she had most longed for. Hannah was childless. She longed for a child, and she begged God in her prayers to make her fruitful. Eventually her longing was fulfilled, and she gave birth to a little boy, whom she called Samuel. She must have felt that her deepest desire had been satisfied. But in the journey of the soul, there is always somewhere deeper than the deepest we can discover. Hannah, holding the child of her longing, now desired to express her gratitude, and so she made Samuel over to the service of God. After she had weaned him, she let him go. She gave him up, leaving him in the Temple.

The story goes on to reveal that Hannah would visit Samuel in the Temple every year, and each year she would take with her a little coat she had made for him. Each year it would be a bigger coat than the year before. This story moves me deeply. Amid all the paraphernalia of the Temple sacrifices and the big talk about the people's covenant with their Lord, here is a mother who knows, as only a mother can, that her little boy is growing all the time, and will need a bigger coat each year.

Nature is a mother like that to us, her children. And to the Celtic mind, 'Nature' in all its forms is the embodiment of God himself. We, too, grow out of our coats. We grow out of this year's certainties and fixed positions as surely as we fill up this year's diary. We can perhaps imagine little Samuel protesting each year, as his mother took off the coat he had outgrown and gave him the new one in its place. For those few minutes he must have shivered, and felt very exposed. But Hannah knew that if he didn't put on the bigger coat, by the end of the following year he wouldn't be able to move freely because last year's coat would be far too small for him.

When I fall into new chasms of doubt, or face new depths of loss, I try to remember Samuel. When my Mother–God strips off the outgrown garment, I try to trust that she is doing so to give me new space for my next year's growing. Thus doubt becomes a sacred boundary, rather than a fearful abyss, and loss, though grievous, leads to a new gateway of being.

You might like to reflect on the boundaries of doubt and loss in your own experience, which perhaps you are tempted to deny. Don't deny them. They are not the afflictions of darkness, but angels of light calling you forward, leading you to the coracle that will carry you across the next tides of your life, to all that is still waiting to be discovered – even though that coracle may appear to be sailing on an ocean of tears.

The oil of anointing

Before Moses crossed the boundary of death, he anointed the tribes to prepare them for the crossing into the Promised Land. The same kind of ritual anointing is offered to the sick, or those on the point of death, by the Christian sacrament of anointing.

We can anoint each other in many ways. We can do it literally, with scented oils or ointment, or we can do it by holding another person's hand tenderly as they make a crucial passage on their life's journey – perhaps a child leaving home, a loved one going on a journey or a dying friend. We can even do it through the slightest touch, in passing, given in love to one who has need of it. When we anoint, whether we do it literally or symbolically, we are bestowing blessing. We are affirming our trust that creation means well with us all, and that whatever painful growth and change may lie ahead, it is leading us to Life, not to destruction.

The act of anointing fully acknowledges the pain of the threshold experience, and it in no way condones the harmful intentions or neglect that often bring human beings, or indeed any creatures, to the edges of Life. It blesses the transition across the boundary. It eases the passage through fear and loneliness, by lubricating the way with love. Above all, it speaks the truth of our hearts, that this place of passing is sacred space and that the person being anointed is moving beyond the known and the limited, into the unknown and the infinite.

Are you standing on the boundaries of new growth yourself, right now, or do you know anyone who is? Is someone close to you dying or terminally ill? Is someone struggling with doubt, or facing the disintegration of some security they have depended on? If so you might feel drawn to engage your feelings with their hopes and fears in the form of an anointing ritual of your own devising. It is impossible to overstate how much it means to us, as vulnerable human beings, when someone gives us the gift of genuine, caring companionship at the times when we feel most exposed. Let what you do be simple, and authentic, acknowledging the person's pain or fear, and expressing your own compassion. But let it be holy, too. Let it be memorable and meaningful. In the act of anointing, you are expressing your own trust that what lies beyond the boundary veil is constantly drawing us forward to new possibilities. You are helping someone to climb into that little coracle of trust and set sail upon an uncharted ocean of possibility.

When we stand at the borderlands of our being, we know we are in the presence of Life itself, who speaks an eternal Word: 'Behold, I am making all creation new.'

HORIZONS OF HOMECOMING

One summer we spent our family holiday in a small village on the south coast of Turkey. It was quite a way from the well-trodden tourist trail, and the walk to the beach involved negotiating a long, dry, dusty track through a near-wilderness. The beach, too, had its vagaries. While it stretched out, apparently endlessly, to right and left, in long seams of white sand, it also shelved very steeply into the cool Mediterranean waters, making it less than ideal for children or inexperienced swimmers.

The first time I tried out the sea-bathing was quite a shock. For the first few yards the sea was just a warm, calm, paddling pool, where it was possible to sit and gaze at the view, while the gentle ripples lapped around my toes. I was more than content to enjoy the pleasures of doing just this for quite a while. But it was already clear to me that if I wanted to go deeper, I would have to negotiate a sturdy line of breakers, hurling their foam over the brink of the next steep drop into the deeper water.

I am not a particularly strong swimmer, and breaking waves intimidate me! But I dearly longed to go deeper, and do some real bathing from this lovely beach. So I held my breath and threw myself across the boundary of foam and force. On the other side I discovered that I could still touch the ground, but I was now shoulder-deep in the water. Again, there was a stretch of stable ground – a kind of middle-ability swimming pool to enjoy. I stayed there for a long time, and I could have been tempted not to go any further. For, again, there was a formidable breaker line looming at the edges of this enclosure of relative calm.

Perhaps there is always something deep inside us that calls us on, to pass the next boundary, to cross the next 'chaos causeway', to the full extent of our courage and ability. Eventually I plunged through this second breaker line, which proved to be a good deal more turbulent than the first. On the other side I was out of my depth. I could no longer touch the sand with my toes. I *had* to swim. And I had to entrust myself to the buoyancy of the water itself. It was in this necessary act of trust that I also discovered the water would indeed support me. In fact it would support me far more surely than my own floundering efforts at navigation could do. I had passed through the barrier of fear into a place where I was supported by something infinitely larger and more trustworthy than my own small self. My life, so to speak, was no longer entirely in my own control. Yet it was here, across this new boundary line, that the swimming became truly real and alive – a partnership between the force of the water and the movements of my own body.

I looked out to sea again. And I saw line after line of turbulence, stretching out into the distance, as far as the eye could see. Every breaker line marked the boundary between two different levels of the seabed. The waves were thrown into their boundary fury because they themselves had to adjust to the sudden changes of depth. The boundaries of turbulence marked the boundaries of new depths and new challenges. A strong swimmer might have ventured out across several more of these boundary lines. A boat might have sailed far further. But it seemed, from where I was, that the breaker lines stretched on and out, even to infinity.

Risking the depths of our being

As we have moved through the various stations of this pilgrimage of heart, mind and imagination, we too have been searching out ever new depths of our being, exploring these seven sacred spaces within ourselves and our own experience. The soul's journey, of which this pilgrimage is just one small part of one possible route, has something of the character of life itself. It allows us to begin wherever we are, and to dabble our toes for as long as we wish in the safe space where our survival is assured and there are no serious challenges. We could say this is like our soul's babyhood.

Then, if we desire it and dare it, we can move onto a different stage of our Becoming. Here we are still in control. We have the measure of the visible world around us. We feel safe, in our own identity and within our own limits. This is the adult world, where we live the external existence of our 'ego' selves, coping with life's demands, rising to life's occasions, building our homes, raising our families, forging our careers. It is a completely necessary stage, and one that cannot be bypassed. It is like the shell of the egg of our being. The chick within us, the seed of our eternal reality, needs its ego-shell to survive long enough to reach the maturity needed for hatching into something new.

For most of us, most of the time, this middle ground of living is where we feel comfortable and where we choose to function. Yet it is very much the 'above-ground' world we noticed in chapter 1. It is where we function as individuals in our own strength, and relate to each other in the ways we choose and control. It is not the end of the journey. It is not the 'place of resurrection'. Because, as we well know if we dare to look beyond it, there are more and more breaker lines beckoning us onward, through uncharted seas, towards a horizon that looks like infinity.

To cross a new breaker line, however it presents itself in our lives, demands an act of courage and faith. It will always take us through turbulence to a new depth of our being. In that new depth, we will eventually find ourselves 'out of our depth', and we will then have to trust in powers beyond our own. We will be challenged to trust that the power which holds us means well with us, and that it sustains the totality of creation as well as our own selves. We know that in these new depths our souls will at last begin to find the freedom they long for, but it becomes a collective freedom, and no longer an individual liberty. The further we extend our hearts and our being to the horizons of infinity, the less we can remain just 'I', and the more we become aware of our total interrelatedness with each other and with all creation.

This process will gradually, without our noticing, grow us from 'I alone' into the 'All-One' of creation, which is so beautifully expressed in the Celtic infinite knot, with which we began this journey. The 'chaos boundaries' we must cross, to proceed on our soul's journey, make it a costly undertaking, yet the destination is beyond price. It is nothing less than a homecoming to the original wholeness from which our limited, autonomous selves first sprang, and to which they long to return, to become for ever reconnected with all that is.

Walking with angels?

The Celts recognized, and honoured, the presence of 'angels' in their lives. Angels were considered to be a supernatural extension of the natural world, as well as the personal guardians and guides of each pilgrim through life. Many other spiritual paths likewise seek and respect the support of 'spirit guides' on the journey towards the 'All-One', where all that has become disconnected and fragmented is made whole once more.

Perhaps we all have our own ideas of what an 'angel' might be, and every such picture will be severely limited and inadequate. Yet our pictures can be a help to us, provided that we bear in mind their inevitable limitations. My own 'angel' picture is this:

I see myself making my way through the visible world, mainly in the middle ground of the 'ego-self'. My 'ego' builds itself up and bolsters its own importance, for the sake of my personal survival. It collects possessions, builds walls to protect itself, makes 'exclusive' relationships to keep itself loved, seeks status and recognition. The bigger it gets, the bigger the shadow it casts over the Earth, blocking out the eternal light from the patch of earth it stands on. Logically, if we all allow our ego-selves to grow without question or restraint, we could collectively block out *all* the light. And sometimes the symptoms of our planet's dis-ease would indicate that this is exactly what we are doing.

What happens, however, if we cross the boundaries into the more mature stages of our Becoming? Suppose we do find the courage to risk the leap over the final breaker line to reach the depths where we have to rely on the water itself to support us. Suppose we find the courage to let go our desperate grip on the

'I' we think we are, and trust that in the 'All-One' of recreated wholeness we shall be at once more safe and more free than we can possibly imagine. Then the bulk of our ego-self, and the shadow it casts upon the Earth, would diminish, and eventually disappear.

In my personal picture of the 'angels', I see my 'angel' as a presence of light exactly the same shape as my ego-shadow. She is, as it were, the patch of light that my ego-shadow has displaced from the Earth. The darkness cast by my ego-shadow has a corresponding presence of light in the invisible world, like a jigsaw piece of light and radiance that exactly matches my shadow shape. I can only rediscover my angel to the extent that I am willing to let go of the bulk and baggage of my ego. When this shadow finally disappears completely, my 'angel' will have repossessed the ground she once inhabited, restoring light to where there was darkness. Meanwhile, my angel – the light equivalent of my own dark shadow – is always there, to guide and encourage me to take the next step of faith.

For many people the idea of an 'angel' may be mere fantasy; for others the presence of angels may be something almost palpable. It doesn't really matter how we imagine such presence or what we call it. We don't have to force our imaginations round unnatural bends and twists to take hold of this possibility. Enough, perhaps, simply to be aware that there is an immortal, eternal reality within our own deepest selves – our *true selves* – which is constantly in attendance, like an angel of light, to guide us. We might call it the light of conscience, or the inner compass that keeps us living true. Whatever name we give it, it is beckoning us, and empowering us, to take each new plunge beyond the boundaries of our ego-selves, into the ocean where our true selves are recreated into the wholeness we have lost. It is urging us to travel beyond the horizons that lead us home to our eternal selves.

And there is a very human counterpart to our 'angel', whom the Celts called the *anam cara* or 'soul-friend'. The soul-friend is a companion of our hearts' journey, who will listen lovingly to our own attempts to articulate where we are and how we feel about it. He or she will not judge, advise or direct, but merely accompany us, noticing and pointing out to us the movements within the core of our being, acting as a kind of midwife to the coming to birth of our true self. The gift of soul-friendship is ours for the asking. All we need to do is to look around our circle of friends or acquaintances and notice who, particularly, appears to be 'on our wavelength', sharing something of our personal vision of life, able themselves to draw on a deep well of spiritual wisdom, and whom we feel we can trust with the innermost secrets of our hearts. Having identified such a person, we can then approach them and ask for their companionship at this, the deepest level of our being, and arrange to meet regularly to share the journey. Soul-friendship is a special and sacred relationship. If you take nothing else along with you on your inner journey, consider very seriously the possibility of travelling with a soul-friend.

The challenge of Jubilee

We have walked a path of seven sacred spaces. Each of them has been a place of meeting between the visible and invisible worlds, between the ego-self and the true self deep in our souls. Now we approach the final boundary.

One of our companions on this journey has been Moses – a man who walked the boundaries of the seen and the unseen in powerful and spectacular ways, according to Judaic tradition. The book of Leviticus describes how this man, who spoke with God, takes his people forward beyond the limits of the sacred and significant power of Seven. He leads them to the call of the Sabbath Day, the Sabbatical Year and the Year of Jubilee:

● The Sabbath Day is a call to rest after six days' work. It is also a call to enter, regularly, our own quiet depths and seek the true self that the frenzied world of everyday, largely driven by the needs of the ego-self, can so easily banish from our minds.

- The Sabbatical Year is to be honoured every seventh year, when the land is to rest and renew itself, freed from the burden of crop-yielding, and when debts are to be cancelled, so that human life, and creation itself, can be restored to balance.

- The Year of Jubilee is to be celebrated every fiftieth year, to mark the importance of the completion of seven cycles of seven years. After forty-nine years of the routine of work and rest, of cultivating the visible world while also nourishing the invisible depths within us, the fiftieth year is to be proclaimed a Jubilee.

The desire to live within a natural rhythm of effort and rest, moving between our visible routine and our invisible soul depths, is common to all humanity. If we look more closely at what was demanded by the Judaic law of Jubilee, we may find a surprising resonance within ourselves with all that underlies this universal desire for 'a taste of infinity'.

Jubilee is an image of homecoming:

- It required the people to return to their roots and their family origins. The call to the pilgrim making the inner journey to the true self is also a call back to first beginnings, where we were still at home in the 'All-One' below the tideline of individual consciousness. Part of this journeying may well involve getting in touch with the spiritual pathways of those who have gone before us, and allowing ourselves to be touched by their wisdom. Sabbath, and Jubilee, are expressions of the universal desire for homecoming, to a place where there is wholeness and fulfilment.

- It demanded a rest from labour and a reliance on the simple gathering and sharing of harvest. Creation was to be allowed a season of rest, and every creature was to become a passive partaker of the harvest, trusting in resources beyond its own control. The deeper reaches of our soul-journey ask us, likewise, to let go of the frenzied need for 'doing' and rather to rest in the simplicity of 'Being' – to embrace the waiting time and to let the seeds of eternity ripen within us.

A confident trust in the gift of harvest is only possible if creation's harvest is equally shared by all and there is a real acknowledgment that what the Earth yields is for all Earth-dwellers. To put this into practice is to trust that we have all the mental and physical resources to sustain the whole of life on our planet in well-being and health. What we appear to lack is the spiritual will to desire this Dream. Our desire for universal homecoming, therefore, becomes a passionate and continuous cry for justice and peace – a cry which will not cease until the Dream is made into reality.

We are each called to seek out our own personal vocation in turning the Dream of restored wholeness into a living reality on our planet. When we embrace this call, we are recognizing that our own lives are the most potent 'sacred space' of all. Each one of us lives on the boundary of the visible world of our lived experience, and the invisible world that opens up to us in the core of our being. Every life is a place where the power and the light of eternity is potentially focused. Each life is a flashpoint where a spark of the eternal fire of creation has the power to kindle the fires of justice. Every searching heart is a gateway to the still centre of peace and love around which all creation revolves in balance like the universe of stars and galaxies. To enter the core of our own being is to enter the heart of all creation and to be at home there, where every other creature is seen to be as sacred as we are ourselves.

The individual pilgrimage in search of the true self is only ever authentic when it leads to the point of awareness that all our 'true selves' are living cells within a greater wholeness of complete interrelatedness and interdependence. When we discover our own 'pearl of great price', we will always find it to be one and the same thing as the pearl of great price for all of creation. Having made our pilgrimage of 'seven times seven', having lived our own weeks and years in search of our own deepest truth, we come to the place where our 'alone' becomes the 'All-One' of original wholeness. When we reach this point we glimpse the truth that the existential loneliness, in which we so often feel we are living, is actually leading to a very different kind of true 'Belonging'. Not the Belonging that implies possession, but the Belonging that holds us in ultimate freedom, each true self discovering its meaning in the true self of All.

At the end of our pilgrimage, as we begin to glimpse the beckoning light of our 'place of resurrection', we move beyond the seven times seven of our searching and wandering, loving, losing and labouring. Our focus lengthens, beyond our own orbit, to the needs and longings of all creation, and to the promise of all that still lies beyond the horizon of our perceptions. A big Dream! But in every moment that we live and breathe, we are growing into it, dreaming and *real*-izing our own part in the Dream of all creation, reaching out to each new horizon along the Way that leads us Home.

Picture acknowledgments

CHRISTOPHER HILL PHOTOGRAPHIC
pp. 50–51: Farmhouse on Dooey
Peninsula, Donegal, Ireland

COLLECTIONS
p. 42 and cover image: Drumcliffe high
cross, Co. Sligo, Ireland (*Michael Diggin*)
pp. 56–57: Stone circle, Harthill Moor,
Derbyshire (*Robin Weaver*)
pp. 60–61: Mourne Mts, Co. Down,
Ireland (Image Ireland: *John Scovell*)
pp. 144–145: Loch Cluanie, Glen Shiel,
Scottish Highlands (*Robert Hallmann*)
pp. 158–159: Sunset on the coast near
Portrush, Co. Antrim, Northern Ireland
(*Alain Le Garsmeur*)

MICK SHARP
pp. 2–3: Ring of Brodgar stone circle,
Orkney mainland
p. 6: St Blane's church and monastery,
Kingarth, Isle of Bute
p. 15: St Brynach's Cross, Nevern,
Pembrokeshire (detail)
pp. 34–35: Kilmacduagh round tower,
Co. Galway, Ireland (12th century)
pp. 38–39: Shipwreck memorial cross,
Llanddwyn Island, Newborough, Anglesey,
with St Dwynwen's memorial cross in the
background
pp. 78–79: Sycamore tree, Beverley, East
Yorkshire (*Jean Williamson*)
p. 88: St Brendan's oratory and holy well,
Mt Brandon, Dingle, Co. Kerry, Ireland
p. 95: Boundary stone from the plague
village of Eyam, Derbyshire
p. 103: Dawn of the winter solstice at Llyn
Padarn, Llanberis, Gwynedd, Wales (*Jean
Williamson*)
p. 112: Aberfalls, Aber, Gwynedd, Wales
(*Jean Williamson*)
pp. 134–135: Old pilgrim causeway
to Holy Island, Northumberland (*Jean
Williamson*)
pp. 138–139: Meavy ford and stepping
stones, Dartmoor, Devon (*Jean Williamson*)

pp. 166–167: Ring of Brodgar henge and
stone circle, Orkney mainland (*Jean
Williamson*)

NICK ROUS
pp. 68–69: Black cottages, Garinan, Isle
of Lewis
pp. 84–85: Bluebells, Wytham Wood,
Oxfordshire
pp. 152–153: Gravestones at Eynsham,
Oxfordshire

SUPERSTOCK
pp. 174–175: Kayaking

TELEGRAPH COLOUR LIBRARY
pp. 30–31: Cross-section of tree trunk
(*Duncan Smith*)
pp. 108–109: Birch trees (*Jan Tove
Johansson*)
pp. 118–119: Autumn countryside,
Gloucestershire (*Peter Adams*)
pp. 126–127: Water tumbling over rocks
(*HH*)

WOODFALL WILD IMAGES
pp. 22–23: Summer Isles, Achiltibuie
(*Val Corbett*)
pp. 72–73: Beinn Eighe, Torridon,
Scottish Highlands (*Alan Gordon*)
p. 182: Giant's Causeway, Co. Antrim,
Northern Ireland (*David Woodfall*)